I0797784
THIS BELONGS TO

I am Someone Who...

2000+ fill-in questions.
Get to know more about yourself.

This edition published by Piccadilly (USA) Inc.

10 9 8 7 6 5 4 3 2 1

Made in China

ISBN: 978-1-48897-517-2

Who Are You Really?

It's a question that echoes through time—sharp, raw, and endlessly relevant. It's more than a name or a title, more than your job, your history, or your highlight reel. It's the question that lives beneath the noise. It's the heartbeat under the surface. It's the late-night whisper that lingers long after the world goes quiet. Not the version you've curated, or the one people assume, but the real you—messy, growing, present.

You've probably heard the question before—sung loud with defiance and soul by The Who in their iconic 1978 song: "Who are you? Who, who, who, who?" It's a line that strikes a nerve because it asks what we often avoid. Beneath the layers we build to navigate the world, beneath the stories we repeat, lies the root of it all—our identity.

This book is your invitation to uncover that identity sentence by sentence. Not to define yourself once and for all, but to explore yourself with honesty and curiosity. With thoughtful enlightenment. Because sometimes the deepest clarity doesn't come from finding the "right" answer, but from asking the right kind of questions.

Each sentence you write beginning with **"I am someone who..."** is a breadcrumb leading back to yourself. This is an exercise in thoughtful enlightenment—gently peeling back the layers, exploring what's real, what's changing, and what's always been. It's about noticing the way you move through the world, how you feel when you're alone with your thoughts, and the values that rise up when everything else falls away.

Maybe you're someone who forgives too easily. Or holds on too long. Maybe you're someone who believes in love after loss. Someone who laughs when it's wildly inappropriate. Someone who's still learning how to rest. Or someone who secretly dreams of starting over.

Whatever comes out, let it. There are no wrong answers here. Only real ones.

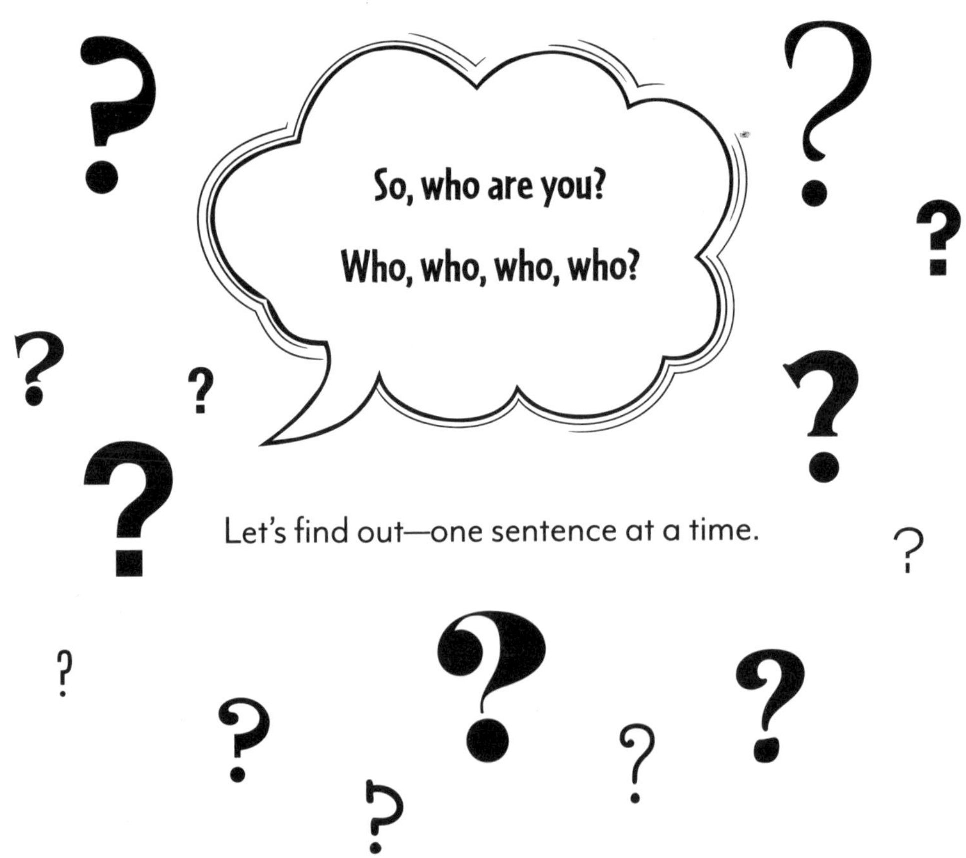

Word Association Warm-Up

Before we dive deep into self-exploration, let's begin with a simple yet powerful exercise to spark your creativity and tap into your subconscious. This activity is designed to loosen up your thoughts and get your pen moving without overthinking.

How it works:

 Read the word or phrase provided.

 Write down the first word, thought, or image that comes to mind. Don't censor yourself—there are no right or wrong answers.

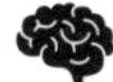 Think about WHY. Let yourself explore the emotions, images, or memories those words unearthed—reflect on the echoes they left behind and what you felt, remembered, or saw in your mind's eye.

 If you feel inspired, expand on that thought. Jot down a sentence, a memory, or a feeling associated with it. Remember, the goal is to let your thoughts flow freely. This exercise helps uncover hidden associations and sets the tone for deeper introspection.

> **"Words mean more than what is set down on paper. It takes the human voice to infuse them with deeper meaning."**

-Maya Angelou

Let's Begin

Sharp

Black sheep

Pushover

Diary

Backup plan

Fierce

Complacent

Metamorphosis

Pop quiz

Feeling myself

Thunder

Glow in the dark

Unfiltered

Invisible

Permission

Reset

Mask

Bad habits

Monday

Anchor

Glitter

Transformation

Garden

Vacation

Digital detox

Birthday

Sunset

1. I am someone who thinks ______________________________

______________________________ is overrated.

2. I am someone who loves to ______________________________

______________________________ when it rains.

3. I am someone who never takes ______________________________

______________________________ for granted.

4. I am someone who hopes for ______________________________

______________________________.

5. I am someone who understands the value of ______________________________

______________________________.

6. I am someone who knows ______________________________

______________________________ is the best thing you can do for yourself.

7. I am someone who never gets enough ______________________________

______________________________.

8. I am someone who loves spending time with ______________________________

______________________________.

9. I am someone who is picky when it comes to ______________________________

______________________________.

10. I am someone who daydreams about ______________________________

______________________________.

11. I am someone who wants more ______________________________

______________________________ in my life.

12. I am someone who loves to be surrounded by ______________________________

____.

13. I am someone who thinks ____

____ is priceless.

14. I am someone who appreciates ____

____.

15. I am someone who ____

____ when I get upset.

16. I am someone who would never be caught doing ____________________________

____.

17. I am someone who values ____

____ in relationships.

18. I am someone who smiles when ____

____.

19. I am someone who splurges on ____

____.

20. I am someone who feels out of place when _________________________________

____.

21. I am someone who never wants anyone to feel ______________________________

____.

22. I am someone who is always thinking about _________________________________

____.

23. I am someone who doesn't pay attention to ______________________________.

24. I am someone who defines success as ______________________________.

25. I am someone who believes in ______________________________.

26. I am someone who never underestimates the power of ______________________________.

27. I am someone who wants to learn more about ______________________________.

28. I am someone who feels happiest when ______________________________.

29. I am someone who gets emotional when ______________________________.

30. I am someone who has sacrificed ______________________________.

31. I am someone who wants to be described as ______________________________.

32. I am someone who hates when ______________________________.

33. I am someone who usually forgets ______________________________.

34. I am someone who sees myself as ______________________________

______________________________.

35. I am someone who could eat ______________________________

______________________________ almost everyday.

36. I am someone who feels nostalgic when ______________________________

______________________________.

37. I am someone who ______________________________

______________________________ reading.

38. I am someone who cherishes ______________________________

______________________________.

39. I am someone who prioritizes ______________________________

______________________________ in relationships.

40. I am someone who ______________________________

______________________________ when faced with a challenge.

41. I am someone who is never satisfied when it comes to ______________________________

______________________________.

42. I am someone who speaks my mind about ______________________________

______________________________.

43. I am someone who never wants to lose ______________________________

______________________________.

44. I am someone who is unique because ______________________________

______________________________.

45. I am someone who feels insecure about ______________________________

______________________________.

46. I am someone who wants to make a difference by ______________________________

______________________________.

47. I am someone who ______________________________

______________________________ before I go to sleep.

48. I am someone who wishes they could meet ______________________________

______________________________.

49. I am someone who is hard on myself when it comes to ______________________________

______________________________.

50. I am someone who thinks ______________________________

is more important than ______________________________.

51. I am someone who needs to let go of ______________________________

______________________________.

52. I am someone who has to juggle ______________________________

______________________________.

53. I am someone who thinks life is too short to ______________________________

______________________________.

54. I am someone who usually sings in ______________________________

______________________________.

55. I am someone who has a hidden talent of ______________________________

______________________________.

56. I am someone who has a hard time making a decision when it comes to ______

______.

57. I am someone who doesn't waste time on ______

______ almost everyday.

58. I am someone who gets shy when ______

______.

59. I am someone who has very strong opinions about ______

______.

60. I am someone who will never get tired of ______

______.

61. I am someone who has fond memories of ______

______ in relationships.

62. I am someone who overthinks when it comes to ______

______.

6. I am someone who craves ______

______.

64. I am someone who has a phobia of ______

______.

65. I am someone who is always trying to ______

______.

66. I am someone who doesn't take no for an answer when ______

______.

67. I am someone who needs ____________________

____________________ to feel safe.

68. I am someone who always has a good time when ____________________

____________________.

69. I am someone who is looking for ____________________

____________________.

70. I am someone who cares about ____________________

____________________.

71. I am someone who is invested in ____________________

____________________.

72. I am someone who tries not to ____________________

____________________.

73. I am someone who feels valued when ____________________

____________________.

74. I am someone who responds negatively to ____________________

____________________.

75. I am someone who makes mistakes but ____________________

____________________.

76. I am someone who has a bad habit of ____________________

____________________.

77. I am someone who thinks kindness ____________________

____________________.

78. I am someone who is often called ____

____ by family or friends.

79. I am someone who is notorious for ____

____.

80. I am someone who is afraid of being ____

____.

81. I am someone who admires ____

____.

82. I am someone who needs to spend more time ____

____.

83. I am someone who sometimes forgets ____

____ in relationships.

84. I am someone who never lets ____

____ bother me.

85. I am someone who can't go a day without ____

____.

86. I am someone who will not tolerate ____

____.

87. I am someone who is curious about ____

____.

88. I am someone who determined to ____

____.

89. I am someone who is unlikely to ______________________________

______________________________.

90. I am someone who always tries to get out of ______________________________

______________________________.

91. I am someone who usually can be found at ______________________________

______________________________.

92. I am someone who thinks secrets are ______________________________

______________________________.

93. I am someone who loves to relax by ______________________________

______________________________.

94. I am someone who openly shares ______________________________

about myself because I want others to ______________________________

95. I am someone who seeks ______________________________

______________________________.

96. I am someone who collects ______________________________

______________________________.

97. I am someone who spends too much time ______________________________

______________________________.

98. I am someone who wants to understand how ______________________________

______________________________.

99. I am someone who doesn't like to use the word ______________________________

______________________________.

100. I am someone who probably will never ____

____.

101. I am someone who is always researching ____

____.

102. I am someone who stresses about ____

____.

103. I am someone who goes out of my way to ____

____.

104. I am someone who imagines what it would be like to ____

____.

105. I am someone who would jeopardize my ____

for ____.

106. I am someone who takes ____

____ very seriously.

107. I am someone who gets squeamish when ____

____.

108. I am someone who has taken a chance on ____

____.

109. I am someone who will never compromise my ____

____.

110. I am someone who can't hide my emotions when ____

____.

111. I am someone who regrets ______________________________

______________________________.

112. I am someone who could spend all day ______________________________

______________________________.

113. I am someone who has a hard time trusting ______________________________

______________________________.

114. I am someone who freaks out when ______________________________

______________________________.

115. I am someone who is obsessed with ______________________________

______________________________.

116. I am someone who will never turn down a ______________________________

______________________________.

117. I am someone who has outgrown ______________________________

______________________________.

118. I am someone who takes their time ______________________________

______________________________.

119. I am someone who appreciates ______________________________

______________________________.

120. I am someone who loves to ______________________________

______________________________ on sunny days.

121. I am someone who tries hard to ______________________________

______________________________.

122. I am someone who has trouble explaining ______________________________

______________________________.

123. I am someone who has a firm grasp on ______________________________

______________________________.

124. I am someone who is trying to keep the promise I made to myself of ______________

______________________________.

125. I am someone who loves to take advantage of a good ______________________

______________________________.

126. I am someone who hates to share ______________________________

______________________________ about myself.

127. I am someone who wonders about ______________________________

______________________________.

128. I am someone who likes to create ______________________________

______________________________ very seriously.

129. I am someone who thinks ______________________________

is too ______________________________.

130. I am someone who tries not to worry about ______________________________

______________________________.

131. I am someone who feels alive when ______________________________

______________________________.

132. I am someone who has a hard time believing ______________________________

______________________________.

133. I am someone who hopes to visit ______

and see ______.

134. I am someone who has little patience for ______

______.

135. I am someone who thinks surprises are ______

______.

136. I am someone who loves to have fun by ______

______.

137. I am someone who spends less time doing ______

now than I used to because ______.

138. I am someone who is trying to heal from ______

______.

139. I am someone who wants the best for ______

______.

140. I am someone who doesn't concern myself with ______

because it ______.

141. I am someone who will always choose ______

over ______.

142. I am someone who sometimes pretends ______

______ on sunny days.

143. I am someone who has had a nightmare about ______

______.

144. I am someone who has always had to ______________________________

______________________________ for myself.

145. I am someone who doesn't like to talk about ______________________________

______________________________.

146. I am someone who doesn't mind wasting time if I'm ______________________________

______________________________.

147. I am someone who keeps trying to ______________________________

in an effort to ______________________________.

148. I am someone who is working on improving ______________________________

______________________________.

149. I am someone who feels strong when ______________________________

______________________________.

150. I am someone who thinks the world needs more ______________________________

______________________________.

151. I am someone who is skilled at ______________________________

______________________________.

152. I am someone who wants to help others ______________________________

______________________________.

153. I am someone who is grateful for ______________________________

______________________________.

154. I am someone who could benefit from some ______________________________

______________________________.

155. I am someone who can be vulnerable when ____

____.

156. I am someone who prefers to ____

instead of ____.

157. I am someone who thinks the world needs less ____

____.

158. I am someone who thinks people should have more meaningful conversations about

____.

159. I am someone who feels incomplete without ____

____.

160. I am someone who loves discovering new ____

____.

161. I am someone who believes in the philosophy of ______________________________________

____.

162. I am someone who thinks money is wasted on ____

____.

163. I am someone who won't apologize for ____

____.

164. I am someone who has outgrown ____

____.

165. I am someone who wants to invest in ____

____.

166. I am someone who always brings ______________________________

______________________________ to the table.

167. I am someone who has perfected the art of ______________________________

______________________________.

168. I am someone who will probably end up ______________________________

______________________________.

169. I am someone who doesn't want to ______________________________

to get ______________________________.

170. I am someone who gives myself permission to ______________________________

______________________________.

171. I am someone who enjoys ______________________________

______________________________ in others.

172. I am someone who is motivated by ______________________________

______________________________.

173. I am someone who wants to stay away from ______________________________

______________________________.

174. I am someone who pushes boundaries when I ______________________________

______________________________.

175. I am someone who likes to test my limits by ______________________________

______________________________.

176. I am someone who aspires to ______________________________

______________________________.

177. I am someone who tries to attract good vibes by ______________________________

____.

178. I am someone who is ____

____ at keeping secrets.

179. I am someone who has had ____

____ relationships

180. I am someone who has a love/hate relationship with _____________________

____.

181. I am someone who would rate my life currently on a scale of 1-10 as ___________

____.

182. I am someone who often channels my inner ________________________________

____.

183. I am someone who ____

____ thinks outside the box.

184. I am someone who believes ____

____ is one of my best attributes.

185. I am someone who freak out if I encountered ______________________________

____.

186. I am someone who does their best to live life ______________________________

____ on sunny days.

187. I am someone who has a reputation for __________________________________

____.

188. I am someone who hopes tomorrow will ______________________________

____.

189. I am someone who would be willing to ______________________________

for ____.

190. I am someone who thinks trends are ______________________________

____.

191. I am someone who doesn't mind waiting for ______________________________

____.

192. I am someone who prefers to spend more time doing ______________________________

instead of ____.

193. I am someone who will pay more money for ______________________________

____.

194. I am someone who thinks second chances are ______________________________

____.

195. I am someone who makes a big deal out of ______________________________

____.

196. I am someone who is head over heels about ______________________________

____.

197. I am someone who sees themselves as ______________________________

____.

198. I am someone who cherishes the small things in life like ______________________________

____.

199. I am someone who thinks I would be good at ______________________________

______________________________.

200. I am someone who is drawn to ______________________________

______________________________.

201. I am someone who practices ______________________________

______________________________.

202. I am someone who ______________________________

______________________________ is wasted on.

203. I am someone who might overlook ______________________________

______________________________.

204. I am someone who would have a hard time forgiving ______________________________

______________________________.

205. I am someone who is suspicious of ______________________________

______________________________.

206. I am someone who ______________________________

______________________________ to get what I want.

207. I am someone who thinks ______________________________

______________________________ is a vital part of life.

208. I am someone who ______________________________

______________________________ overthinks.

209. I am someone who notices ______________________________

______________________________.

210. I am someone who procrastinates when ______________________________

____.

211. I am someone who dreams of working with ___________________________

____.

212. I am someone who can make people __________________________________

____.

213. I am someone who ____

____ when I get nervous.

214. I am someone who loves the smell of ________________________________

____.

215. I am someone who refuses to lose sleep over ___________________________

____.

216. I am someone who thinks it's more productive to ________________________

instead of ____.

217. I am someone who likes variety when it comes to _________________________

____.

218. I am someone who prefers ____

climate rather than ____.

219. I am someone who takes after my ____

because I ____.

220. I am someone who does not like to take sides when ________________________

____.

221. I am someone who has an open mind when it comes to ______________________

____.

222. I am someone who misses ____

____.

223. I am someone who would never ____

______________________________ no matter how much money you paid me.

224. I am someone who relies heavily on ______________________________________

____.

225. I am someone who thinks ____

is a detriment to ____.

226. I am someone who has lots of opinions about ____________________________

____.

227. I am someone who would describe my inner circle as ______________________

____.

228. I am someone who needs to focus on ____

____.

229. I am someone who makes mistakes but always tries to ______________________

____.

230. I am someone who needs to ____

before I ____.

231. I am someone who has a hard time forgetting about ________________________

____.

232. I am someone who when sick, feels better by ______________________________

____.

233. I am someone who thinks balance means ______________________________

____.

234. I am someone who is learning to accept ______________________________

____.

235. I am someone who thinks ______________________________

____ is rewarding.

236. I am someone who thinks about ______________________________

____ 24/7.

237. I am someone who can always ______________________________

____.

238. I am someone who isn't receptive to ______________________________

____.

239. I am someone who gets butterflies when ______________________________

____.

240. I am someone who sees themselves as ______________________________

____.

241. I am someone who uses their imagination to ______________________________

____.

242. I am someone who wants to prove ______________________________

____ wrong.

243. I am someone who sometimes pretends ______________________________

____.

244. I am someone who has goals that consist of ______________________________

____.

245. I am someone who finds ______________________________

____ daunting.

246. I am someone who describes their sense of style as ______________________________

____.

247. I am someone who wants more ______________________________

and less ____.

248. I am someone who appreciates the simplicity of ______________________________

____.

249. I am someone who is always tempted by ______________________________

____.

250. I am someone who would love to be mentored by ______________________________

____.

251. I am someone who is driven by ______________________________

____.

252. I am someone who was proud of myself when I ______________________________

____.

253. I am someone who thinks ______________________________

____ is funny.

254. I am someone who ______________________________

______________________________ binges on TV shows.

255. I am someone who will never participate in ______________________________

______________________________.

256. I am someone who thinks ______________________________

______________________________ is undervalued in society.

257. I am someone who always tries to sharpen my ______________________________

______________________________.

258. I am someone who is looking forward to ______________________________

______________________________.

259. I am someone who pauses throughout my day to ______________________________

______________________________.

260. I am someone who is hoping for an opportunity to ______________________________

______________________________.

261. I am someone who ______________________________

______________________________ poetry.

262. I am someone who ______________________________

______________________________ music.

263. I am someone who thinks ______________________________

is heroic because ______________________________.

264. I am someone who believes ______________________________

______________________________ is the first step towards personal growth.

265. I am someone who loves to be around ______________________________

____.

266. I am someone who thinks the meaning of life is ______________________________

____.

267. I am someone who deals with hurt by ______________________________

____.

268. I am someone who is often misunderstood because ______________________________

____.

269. I am someone who is always searching for______________________________

____.

270. I am someone who lashes out when I feel ______________________________

____.

271. I am someone who thinks the truth is ______________________________

____.

272. I am someone who loves ______________________________

but hates ____.

273. I am someone who gets impatient when ______________________________

____.

274. I am someone who benefits from ______________________________

____.

275. I am someone who thinks being genuine means ______________________________

____.

276. I am someone who thinks living in the moment is ______________________________

____.

277. I am someone who ____

____ about the future.

278. I am someone who ____

____ about the past.

279. I am someone who always ____

____ when working.

280. I am someone who harbors ____

about ____.

281. I am someone who thinks ____

____ is my spirit animal.

282. I am someone who wants more time to _____________________________

____.

283. I am someone who embodies _______________________________________

____.

284. I am someone who embraces _______________________________________

____.

285. I am someone who could be quoted as saying ________________________

____.

286. I am someone who thinks magic is ___________________________________

____.

287. I am someone who doesn't get along with ______________________________.

288. I am someone who regrets buying ______________________________.

289. I am someone who regrets changing ______________________________.

290. I am someone who is brutally honest about ______________________________.

291. I am someone who would never betray ______________________________.

292. I am someone who thinks there are too many ______________________________.

293. I am someone who thinks there are too few ______________________________.

294. I am someone who is always snacking on ______________________________.

295. I am someone who is always drinking ______________________________.

296. I am someone who describes their family as ______________________________.

297. I am someone who people usually think is ______________________________.

298. I am someone who owes a debt of gratitude to ____

____.

299. I am someone who acknowledges ____

____.

300. I am someone who tries to ____

____ each day.

301. I am someone who wishes ____

____ could walk a mile in my shoes.

302. I am someone who never understood why ____

____ is so popular.

303. I am someone who prefers ____

instead of ____ when I need to unwind.

304. I am someone who thinks sports are ____

____.

305. I am someone who could listen to ____

____ for hours.

306. I am someone who gets sleepy when ____

____.

307. I am someone who thinks ____

____ are pests.

308. I am someone who knows better than to ____

____.

309. I am someone who will ______

if I find out someone ______.

310. I am someone who won't back down from ______

______.

311. I am someone who feels nourished by ______

______.

312. I am someone who can make witty remarks like ______

______.

313. I am someone who would rather live ______

than ______.

314. I am someone who will never beg someone to ______

______.

315. I am someone who could spend all day ______

______.

316. I am someone who seldom ______

but always ______.

317. I am someone who uses ______

______ daily.

318. I am someone who is not proud of the fact I ______

______.

319. I am someone who is good at ______

but not ______.

320. I am someone who feels challenged by ______________________________

____.

321. I am someone who ____

____ mornings.

322. I am someone who ____

____ late nights.

323. I am someone who has the potential to ____________________________

____.

324. I am someone who manages ______________________________________

____.

325. I am someone who thinks big risks are ____________________________

____.

326. I am someone who envisions ______________________________________

____ for my life.

327. I am someone who tries not to complain about ______________________

____.

328. I am someone who approaches ____________________________________

with the mindset ____.

329. I am someone who dares to ______________________________________

____.

330. I am someone who wants to have an adventure that __________________

____.

331. I am someone who hates to be ____

____.

332. I am someone who thinks karma is ____

____.

333. I am someone who takes steps to ensure _____________________________________

____.

334. I am someone who is attracted to ____

____.

335. I am someone who has conquered ____

____.

336. I am someone who ____

____ when I am wrong.

337. I am someone who found ____

____.

338. I am someone who would love to be ____

____ for a day.

339. I am someone who wants to discover ____

____.

340. I am someone who feels protective of ______________________________________

____.

341. I am someone who thinks ____

____ is a scam.

342. I am someone who ______________________________

______________________________ comes second nature to.

343. I am someone who has been rebellious when ______________________________

______________________________.

344. I am someone who loves the quote: ______________________________

______________________________.

345. I am someone who ______________________________

______________________________ feedback.

346. I am someone who describes their outlook on life as ______________________________

______________________________.

347. I am someone who speaks out against ______________________________

______________________________.

348. I am someone who stands up for ______________________________

______________________________.

349. I am someone who describes their hometown as ______________________________

______________________________.

350. I am someone who wants their (love interest) partner to ______________________________

______________________________.

351. I am someone who believes hospitality is ______________________________

______________________________.

352. I am someone who thinks revenge is ______________________________

______________________________.

353. I am someone who could never be described as a ______________________________.

354. I am someone who is old-fashioned when it comes to ______________________________.

355. I am someone who has a more contemporary outlook on ______________________________.

356. I am someone who could watch ______________________________ endlessly.

357. I am someone who is picky about ______________________________.

358. I am someone who tries not to judge ______________________________.

359. I am someone who enjoys watching other people ______________________________.

360. I am someone who finds it hard to thrive when ______________________________.

361. I am someone who frequently eats at ______________________________.

362. I am someone who would describe their favorite food as ______________________________.

363. I am someone who thinks ______________________________ is a good idea.

364. I am someone who wishes they knew how to cook ____________________

____________________.

365. I am someone who loves to cuddle with ____________________

____________________.

366. I am someone who does ____________________

____________________ when I can't sleep.

367. I am someone who ____________________

____________________ when I have a nightmare.

368. I am someone who tries harder when ____________________

____________________.

369. I am someone who gets cranky if ____________________

____________________.

370. I am someone who ____________________

____________________ when I feel lazy.

371. I am someone who needs to do more research about ____________________

because ____________________.

372. I am someone who needs to stop lying to myself about ____________________

____________________.

373. I am someone who will always play ____________________

____________________ on game night.

374. I am someone who owes ____________________

____________________ an apology.

375. I am someone who prefers to ______________________________

______________________________ alone.

376. I am someone who thinks ______________________________

______________________________ is the best thing ever invented.

377. I am someone who ______________________________

______________________________ write a memoir about their life.

378. I am someone who ______________________________

gossip about ______________________________.

379. I am someone who respects ______________________________

because ______________________________.

380. I am someone who wishes they could change their ______________________________

______________________________.

381. I am someone who is encouraged when ______________________________

______________________________.

382. I am someone who could read ______________________________

______________________________ over and over.

383. I am someone who thinks an eye for an eye is ______________________________

______________________________.

384. I am someone who can be resourceful like the time I ______________________________

______________________________.

385. I am someone who thinks ______________________________

______________________________ gets better with age.

386. I am someone who changes their mind about ______________________

______________________ often.

387. I am someone who thinks ______________________

______________________ is fun.

388. I am someone who ______________________

______________________ trauma.

389. I am someone who is totally transparent about the fact ______________________

______________________.

390. I am someone who thinks jealousy is ______________________

______________________.

391. I am someone who doesn't like to feel ______________________

because it makes me ______________________.

392. I am someone who ______________________

______________________ when I have a setback.

393. I am someone who thinks trying to fit in is ______________________

______________________.

394. I am someone who is less interested in ______________________

______________________ the older I get.

395. I am someone who is more interested in ______________________

______________________ the older I get.

396. I am someone who practices ______________________

______________________.

397. I am someone who ______________________________

______________________________ at parties.

398. I am someone who ______________________________

______________________________ on a first date.

399. I am someone who has an unpopular opinion of ______________________________

______________________________ because of

400. I am someone who has trouble controlling ______________________________

when ______________________________.

401. I am someone who likes to ______________________________

______________________________ on weekends.

402. I am someone who think Mondays are ______________________________

______________________________.

403. I am someone who ______________________________

______________________________ when I am afraid.

404. I am someone who ______________________________

______________________________ when I get anxious.

405. I am someone who ______________________________

______________________________ when I get nervous.

406. I am someone who would be perfect for the role of ______________________________

in the movie ______________________________.

407. I am someone who had the most memorable birthday when ______________________________

______________________________.

408. I am someone who ______________________________

______________________________ when I get bad news.

409. I am someone who uses ______________________________

______________________________ as a coping mechanism.

410. I am someone who thinks journaling is ______________________________

______________________________.

411. I am someone who is a fan of ______________________________

______________________________.

412. I am someone who loves to hang out ______________________________

______________________________.

413. I am someone who would never listen to advice from ______________________________

______________________________.

414. I am someone who received their best advice from ______________________________

______________________________.

415. I am someone who wants to decode the mystery of ______________________________

______________________________.

416. I am someone who has never ______________________________

______________________________.

417. I am someone who plans on ______________________________

______________________________ one day.

418. I am someone who gets awkward when ______________________________

______________________________.

419. I am someone who finds ______________________________

______________________________ challenging.

420. I am someone who plays it safe when ______________________________

______________________________.

421. I am someone who wants to improve their ______________________________

______________________________.

422. I am someone who hopes to manifest ______________________________

______________________________.

423. I am someone who is stubborn when it comes to ______________________________

______________________________.

424. I am someone who thinks ______________________________

______________________________ was the most valuable lesson history could teach us.

425. I am someone who loves quality time with ______________________________

______________________________.

426. I am someone who misses ______________________________

if ______________________________.

427. I am someone who describes their motto as ______________________________

______________________________.

428. I am someone who thinks ______________________________

______________________________ is a joke.

429. I am someone who doesn't have a sense of humor about ______________________________

______________________________.

430. I am someone who wants others to appreciate ______________________

more because ______________________.

431. I am someone who has felt overlooked before when ______________________

______________________.

432. I am someone who gets complimented on my ______________________

______________________.

433. I am someone who has felt most valued when ______________________

______________________.

434. I am someone who ______________________

______________________ hustles.

435. I am someone who finds it hard to respect ______________________

______________________.

436. I am someone who goes to ______________________

______________________ when I need advice.

437. I am someone who gets emotional when ______________________

______________________.

438. I am someone who describes their spirituality as ______________________

______________________.

439. I am someone who grew up ______________________

______________________.

440. I am someone who wants their life to reflect ______________________

______________________.

441. I am someone who never accepts ______________________________

____.

442. I am someone who wants to volunteer ______________________________

____.

443. I am someone who ______________________________

______________________________ when I get bored.

444. I am someone who takes a long time to ______________________________

____.

445. I am someone who ______________________________

______________________________ when I need to unwind.

446. I am someone who sounds like a ______________________________

______________________________ when I laugh.

447. I am someone who doesn't mind waiting for ______________________________

____.

448. I am someone who feels guilty when ______________________________

____.

449. I am someone who spends more time ______________________________

than ____.

450. I am someone who defines happiness as ______________________________

____.

451. I am someone who would ______________________________

______________________________ again if given a chance.

452. I am someone who could never have a career as a ______________________________

______________________________.

453. I am someone who always thought of ______________________________

______________________________ as a dream job.

454. I am someone who feels deeply connected to ______________________________

______________________________.

455. I am someone who had a great idea when ______________________________

______________________________.

456. I am someone who likes to do ______________________________ less often and

______________________________ more often.

457. I am someone who loves the weird food combination of ______________________________

combined with ______________________________.

458. I am someone who ______________________________

______________________________ positive affirmations.

459. I am someone who takes ______________________________

______________________________ personally.

460. I am someone who would put ______________________________

______________________________ in a time capsule for future generations to find.

461. I am someone who ______________________________

______________________________ travel to space.

462. I am someone who ______________________________

______________________________ gives me a sense of satisfaction.

463. I am someone who has achieved ____

____.

464. I am someone who recently decided to ______________________________________

____.

465. I am someone who sees myself ____

____ in the next 10 years.

466. I am someone who is influenced by ____

____.

467. I am someone who is ____

____ than most people.

468. I am someone who exaggerates when ____

____.

469. I am someone who feels ____

____ about my body.

470. I am someone who was resilient when ____

____.

471. I am someone who refers to my childhood as __________________________________

____.

472. I am someone who has a ____

____ outlook on life.

473. I am someone who has values and morals that consist of ______________________

____.

474. I am someone who clashes with ______________________________

____.

475. I am someone who needs to get ______________________________

____ off their chest.

476. I am someone who enjoys the ______________________________

____ in life.

477. I am someone who has ______________________________

____ in public before.

478. I am someone who would never ______________________________

____ in public.

479. I am someone who is currently focusing on ______________________________

____.

480. I am someone who has had a history of ______________________________

____.

481. I am someone who is tackling ______________________________

______________________________________ as one of my big projects.

482. I am someone who limits ______________________________

____ in my daily life.

483. I am someone who can be excessive with ______________________________

____.

484. I am someone who wants to reconnect with ______________________________

____.

485. I am someone who advocates for ______________________________

______________________________.

486. I am someone who always wanted to study ______________________________

______________________________.

487. I am someone who hates to wear ______________________________

______________________________.

488. I am someone who thinks ______________________________

______________________________ is pointless.

489. I am someone who has lots of experience ______________________________

______________________________.

490. I am someone who feels like ______________________________

______________________________ sometimes holds me back.

491. I am someone who other people describe as ______________________________

______________________________.

492. I am someone who ______________________________

______________________________ stands out in a crowd.

493. I am someone who is talented at ______________________________

______________________________.

494. I am someone who has a celebrity crush on ______________________________

______________________________.

495. I am someone who once got out of a sticky situation by ______________________________

______________________________.

496. I am someone who thinks ______________________________

______________________________ is romantic.

497. I am someone who doesn't fuss over ______________________________

______________________________.

498. I am someone who doesn't interfere with ______________________________

______________________________.

499. I am someone who has too many ______________________________

______________________________.

500. I am someone who has too little ______________________________

______________________________.

501. I am someone who would never have a ______________________________

______________________________ relationship.

502. I am someone who ______________________________

______________________________ gives people more than one chance.

503. I am someone who will stop talking to you if ______________________________

______________________________.

504. I am someone who surrounds themselves with ______________________________

______________________________.

505. I am someone who admires ______________________________

______________________________ in others.

506. I am someone who seeks validation from ______________________________

______________________________.

507. I am someone who thinks money is ______________________________

____.

508. I am someone who strives to ______________________________

____ for the planet.

509. I am someone who has experimented with ______________________________

____.

510. I am someone who learned the hard way about ______________________________

____.

511. I am someone who grew up ______________________________

____.

512. I am someone who thinks ______________________________

______________________________ is unattractive in a person.

513. I am someone who is always saying the word ______________________________

____.

514. I am someone who is ______________________________

____ at multitasking.

515. I am someone who is/was a member of ______________________________

____.

516. I am someone who has big plans for ______________________________

____.

517. I am someone who has considered taking ______________________________

____.

518. I am someone who hates the color ______________________________

____.

519. I am someone who ______________________________

____ social media.

520. I am someone who believes ______________________________

_____________________________________ is destroying humanity.

521. I am someone who wants to be a good influence on ______________

____.

522. I am someone who doesn't take ______________________________

____ too seriously.

523. I am someone who thinks pranks are ______________________________

____.

524. I am someone who will never give up on ______________________________

____.

525. I am someone who always wanted to ______________________________

____ but was too scared.

526. I am someone who ______________________________

____ care of themselves.

527. I am someone who wishes they had more ______________________________

____.

528. I am someone who hopes to pass down ______________________________

to ____.

529. I am someone who would ______________________________

______________________________ if I won the lottery.

530. I am someone who is still searching for ______________________________

______________________________.

531. I am someone who thinks ______________________________

______________________________ when I look in the mirror.

532. I am someone who wants to share ______________________________

______________________________ with the world.

533. I am someone who can be weird at times when I ______________________________

______________________________.

534. I am someone who thinks fate is ______________________________

______________________________.

535. I am someone who made the biggest mistake of my life when ______________________________

______________________________.

536. I am someone who thinks ______________________________

______________________________ are lucky.

537. I am someone who looks forward to the day ______________________________

______________________________.

538. I am someone who has the nickname ______________________________

______________________________.

539. I am someone who feels refreshed when ______________________________

______________________________.

540. I am someone who is thankful for ____________________

____________________ in my life.

541. I am someone who learned ____________________

from ____________________.

542. I am someone who wants to improve ____________________

____________________ about myself.

543. I am someone who ____________________

____________________ more than once a day.

544. I am someone who ____________________

____________________ when I feel sick.

545. I am someone who ____________________

____________________ when someone tickles me.

546. I am someone who envisions their ideal life as ____________________

____________________.

547. I am someone who loves ____________________

____________________ about myself.

548. I am someone who describes my instincts as ____________________

____________________.

549. I am someone who ____________________

____________________ surprises.

550. I am someone who tries to hide ____________________

____________________ from other people.

551. I am someone who loves ______________________________

______________________________ about my life.

552. I am someone who ______________________________

______________________________ their comfort zone.

553. I am someone who could add more joy to my life if I'd ______________________________

______________________________.

554. I am someone who expresses themselves by ______________________________

______________________________.

555. I am someone who feels ______________________________

______________________________ about where I live.

556. I am someone who feels ______________________________

______________________________ about my heritage.

557. I am someone who wants to go back in time so I can ______________________________

______________________________.

558. I am someone who was good at ______________________________

______________________________ in school.

559. I am someone who was bad at ______________________________

______________________________ in school.

560. I am someone who needs a break from ______________________________

______________________________.

561. I am someone who misses ______________________________

______________________________ from my childhood.

562. I am someone who has an unpopular opinion about ______________________________

____.

563. I am someone who has a special ability to ______________________________

____.

564. I am someone who has always wanted to ______________________________

for my ____.

565. I am someone who describes their self-esteem as ______________________________

____.

566. I am someone who wouldn't mind being stuck on a desert island with ______________

____.

567. I am someone who uses ____

____ as a coping mechanism.

568. I am someone who tried ____

and failed but learned ____.

569. I am someone who thinks communication is ______________________________

____.

570. I am someone who always carries ______________________________________

____ with me.

571. I am someone who has ____

in common with ____.

572. I am someone who loves to imagine one day I'll ______________________________

____.

573. I am someone who spends a typical evening doing ____

____.

574. I am someone who is usually on the fence about ____

____.

575. I am someone who thinks my name is ____

____.

576. I am someone who ____

____ skipped school.

577. I am someone who has had a bad experience with ____

____.

578. I am someone who has a poor opinion of ____

____.

579. I am someone who has a favorable opinion of ____

____.

580. I am someone who has had a good experience with ____

____.

581. I am someone who thinks ____

____ knows me best.

582. I am someone who has ____

____ enemies.

583. I am someone who covets ____

____ as my dream car.

584. I am someone who ____________________

____________________ playlists.

585. I am someone who got ____________________

____________________ grades in school.

586. I am someone who hated participating in ____________________

____________________ in school.

587. I am someone who ____________________

____________________ siblings.

588. I am someone who ____________________

____________________ my parents.

589. I am someone who thinks ____________________

____________________ feels like a roller coaster.

590. I am someone who views ____________________

____________________ as the best part of my day.

591. I am someone who views ____________________

____________________ as the worst part of my day.

592. I am someone who could teach a person how to ____________________

____________________.

593. I am someone who barely survived ____________________

____________________.

594. I am someone who crushed it when ____________________

____________________.

595. I am someone who is good at playing ______________________________

______________________________.

596. I am someone who is bad at playing ______________________________

______________________________.

597. I am someone who prefers alternatives to ______________________________

______________________________.

598. I am someone who ______________________________

______________________________ soda.

599. I am someone who ______________________________

______________________________ sweet tooth.

600. I am someone who ______________________________

______________________________ mood swings.

601. I am someone who always buys ______________________________

______________________________ at the movies.

602. I am someone who ______________________________

______________________________ exercises.

603. I am someone who has a membership to ______________________________

______________________________.

604. I am someone who ______________________________

______________________________ keeps me calm.

605. I am someone who tries to live by the rule: ______________________________

______________________________.

606. I am someone who has doubts about ______________________________

______________________________.

607. I am someone who thinks the best thing a person can do for themselves is ______________

______________________________.

608. I am someone who is ______________________________

______________________________ of the dark.

609. I am someone who ______________________________

______________________________ scary movies.

610. I am someone who ______________________________

______________________________ game shows.

611. I am someone who could be described as ______________________________

introverted and ______________________________ extroverted.

612. I am someone who is ______________________________

______________________________ photogenic.

613. I am someone who got into trouble when ______________________________

______________________________.

614. I am someone who ______________________________

______________________________ journaling.

615. I am someone who ______________________________

______________________________ church.

616. I am someone who has traveled to ______________________________

______________________________.

617. I am someone who thinks astrology is ______________________________

____.

618. I am someone who ____

____ piercings.

619. I am someone who ____

____ somebody famous.

620. I am someone who ____

____ keeps me up at night.

621. I am someone who compares themselves to the fictional character ______________

____.

622. I am someone who is concerned about _____________________________

____ of the world.

623. I am someone who daydreams about punching _________________________

____ in the face.

624. I am someone who needs a resolution for ___________________________

____.

625. I am someone who feels alone when _______________________________

____.

626. I am someone who still needs to heal emotionally from __________________

____.

627. I am someone who ____

____ grudges.

628. I am someone who donates ____________________

to ____________________.

629. I am someone who describes their support system as ____________________

____________________.

630. I am someone who recharges by ____________________

____________________.

631. I am someone who uses the app ____________________

____________________ more than any other app on my phone.

632. I am someone who treats themselves to ____________________

____________________ often.

633. I am someone who has a bad habit of ____________________

____________________.

634. I am someone who prefers my hair to be ____________________

____________________.

635. I am someone who thinks cats are ____________________

____________________.

636. I am someone who thinks dogs are ____________________

____________________.

637. I am someone who thinks hugs are ____________________

____________________.

638. I am someone who thinks holding hands is ____________________

____________________.

639. I am someone who can always be trusted to ______________________________

____.

640. I am someone who handles setbacks ______________________________

____.

641. I am someone who would describe the most important lesson I've learned so far as ____

____.

642. I am someone who handles conflict by ______________________________

____.

643. I am someone who shows appreciation by ______________________________

____.

644. I am someone who ______________________________

______________________ when I want to break the ice with someone new I meet.

645. I am someone who is critical of myself when it comes to ______________________

____.

646. I am someone who describes my long-term goals as ______________________

____.

647. I am someone who describes my short-term goals as ______________________

____.

648. I am someone who gives back to my community by ______________________

____.

649. I am someone who enjoys spending quality time with my family by doing __________

____.

650. I am someone who feels unprepared for ______________________________

____.

651. I am someone who has a big pet peeve ______________________________

____.

652. I am someone who has won ______________________________

____.

653. I am someone who participated in ______________________________

____.

654. I am someone who has worn a costume that was ______________________________

____.

655. I am someone who is trying to manifest ______________________________

____.

656. I am someone who wants to reconnect with ______________________________

____.

657. I am someone who might ______________________________

____ on a first date.

658. I am someone who will probably ______________________________

you instead of ____ you.

659. I am someone who is usually most comfortable wearing ______________________________

____.

660. I am someone who describes their lifestyle as ______________________________

____.

661. I am someone who is always trying to maintain ______________________________
____.

662. I am someone who might be ______________________________
______________________________ if someone played a prank on me.

663. I am someone who would ______________________________
______________________________ if I get accused of something I didn't do.

664. I am someone who is a ______________________________
______________________________ judge of people and character.

665. I am someone who can become annoying when ______________________________
____.

666. I am someone who was sheltered from ______________________________
______________________________ growing up.

667. I am someone who tries not to give into ______________________________
____.

668. I am someone who gets embarrassed when ______________________________
____.

669. I am someone who ______________________________
______________________________ gives/giving advice to other people.

670. I am someone who ______________________________
______________________________ debating people on topics I feel strongly about.

671. I am someone who has never ______________________________
____.

672. I am someone who feels queasy when ______________________________.

673. I am someone who will never stop trying to ______________________________.

674. I am someone who would love to be a contestant on ______________________________.

675. I am someone who ______________________________ the lottery.

676. I am someone who ______________________________ to gamble.

677. I am someone who thinks ______________________________ is the most beautiful place on earth.

678. I am someone who is currently bettering myself by ______________________________.

679. I am someone who ______________________________ judges others.

680. I am someone who feels like they're running out of time to ______________________________.

681. I am someone who puts too much pressure on themselves when ______________________________.

682. I am someone who believes mental health ______________________________.

683. I am someone who thinks ______________________________

______________________________ is the best feeling in the world.

684. I am someone who loves to explore ______________________________

______________________________.

685. I am someone who might ______________________________

______________________________ in a crowded elevator.

686. I am someone who uses sarcasm ______________________________

______________________________.

687. I am someone who was born in ______________________________

______________________________.

688. I am someone who lives with ______________________________

______________________________.

689. I am someone who seeks ______________________________

from ______________________________.

690. I am someone who loves ______________________________

______________________________ store/shop.

691. I am someone who ______________________________

is actively involved in ______________________________.

692. I am someone who frequently visits ______________________________

______________________________ online.

693. I am someone who draws a line when it comes to ______________________________

______________________________.

694. I am someone who is ______________________

______________________ to get along with.

695. I am someone who goes out of my way to ______________________

______________________.

696. I am someone who thinks tattoos are ______________________

______________________.

697. I am someone who has ______________________

______________________ pairs of shoes.

698. I am someone who juggles ______________________

______________________.

699. I am someone who ______________________

______________________ deep conversations.

700. I am someone who feels ______________________

______________________ sometimes gets in my way of achieving my goals.

701. I am someone who ______________________

______________________ spicy food.

702. I am someone who ______________________

______________________ children.

703. I am someone who could be described in one word, ______________________

______________________.

704. I am someone who could set a world record for ______________________

______________________.

705. I am someone who feels courageous when I ______________________________

____.

706. I am someone who ______________________________

____ video games.

707. I am someone who ______________________________

____ poker.

708. I am someone who would describe my ambition as ______________________________

____.

709. I am someone who would like to get better at ______________________________

____.

710. I am someone who treasures the little things in life like ______________________________

and ____.

711. I am someone who believes my life would feel incomplete without ______________________________

____.

712. I am someone who tries to ______________________________

____ others.

713. I am someone who ______________________________

____ brings out the best in me.

714. I am someone who loves ______________________________

____ holiday.

715. I am someone who ______________________________

____ a makeover.

716. I am someone who spends more money on ______________________

______________________ than most people do.

717. I am someone who spends less money on ______________________

______________________ than most people do.

718. I am someone who is a ______________________

______________________ cook.

719. I am someone who can prepare ______________________

______________________ very well.

720. I am someone who ______________________

______________________ loses track of time.

721. I am someone who has had to overcome ______________________

so I could ______________________.

722. I am someone who loves ______________________

______________________ nature.

723. I am someone who ______________________

______________________ as much as I can.

724. I am someone who ______________________

______________________ can make me drool.

725. I am someone who ______________________

______________________ the ocean.

726. I am someone who ______________________

______________________ the woods.

727. I am someone who ______________________________

______________________________ the last word in an argument.

728. I am someone who has compartmentalized ______________________________

in order to ______________________________.

729. I am someone who has recently become concerned about ______________________________

______________________________.

730. I am someone who was recently made aware of ______________________________

______________________________.

731. I am someone who appreciates my ability to ______________________________

______________________________.

732. I am someone who ______________________________

______________________________ others point of view.

733. I am someone who has always looked up to ______________________________

______________________________.

734. I am someone who has to constantly remind myself ______________________________

______________________________.

735. I am someone who is on a journey to find ______________________________

______________________________.

736. I am someone who ______________________________

______________________________ when I have a bad day.

737. I am someone who ______________________________

______________________________ when I have a good day.

738. I am someone who strives for excellence by ______________________________

______________________________.

739. I am someone who thinks the best piece of advice I could give someone would be ______

______________________________.

740. I am someone who tries to be myself even if it ______________________________

______________________________.

741. I am someone who ______________________________

______________________________ over the speed limit.

742. I am someone who has received ______________________________

______________________________ traffic violations.

743. I am someone who ______________________________

______________________________ hitchhike/hitchhiked.

744. I am someone who ______________________________

______________________________ for directions if I don't know where I am.

745. I am someone who would never travel or visit ______________________________

______________________________.

746. I am someone who wants to see the landmark ______________________________

______________________________.

747. I am someone who thinks ______________________________

______________________________ was an important part of history.

748. I am someone who thinks ______________________________

______________________________ was one of the greatest events in history.

749. I am someone who relates to the superhero/villain ______________________

because ______________________.

750. I am someone who cringes when ______________________

______________________.

751. I am someone who ______________________

______________________ over-exaggerates.

752. I am someone who describes their taste in fashion as ______________________

______________________.

753. I am someone who loves the designer/brand ______________________

______________________.

754. I am someone who ______________________

______________________ thrift stores.

755. I am someone who ______________________

______________________ garage sales.

756. I am someone who describes my personality type as ______________________

______________________.

757. I am someone who can annoy people when I ______________________

______________________.

758. I am someone who focuses on the positive things in my life like ______________________

______________________.

759. I am someone who gets weird cravings when ______________________

______________________.

760. I am someone who ______________________________ when invited to dinner.

761. I am someone who spreads kindness by ______________________________.

762. I am someone who has ______________________________ for a stranger.

763. I am someone who feels led by ______________________________ sometimes.

764. I am someone who ______________________________ when I feel empty.

765. I am someone who has felt the presence of ______________________________ before and it felt like ______________________________.

766. I am someone who never turns down a ______________________________.

767. I am someone who devotes meaningful time to ______________________________.

768. I am someone who could be more open-minded about ______________________________.

769. I am someone who has an injury from ______________________________.

770. I am someone who thinks therapy is ______________________________.

771. I am someone who rescued ______________________________

______________________________.

772. I am someone who never pictured myself ______________________________
but ______________________________.

773. I am someone who avoids ______________________________

______________________________.

774. I am someone who always waits until the last minute to ______________________________

______________________________.

775. I am someone who ______________________________

______________________________ written a love letter.

776. I am someone who has benefitted from ______________________________

______________________________.

777. I am someone who would describe my imagination as ______________________________

______________________________.

778. I am someone who usually wakes up at ______________________________

______________________________ on weekends.

779. I am someone who usually wakes up at ______________________________

______________________________ on weekdays.

780. I am someone who loves the band ______________________________

______________________________.

781. I am someone who loves the singer ______________________________

______________________________.

782. I am someone who loves the architectural style of ______________________________

____.

783. I am someone who ____

____ live in the city.

784. I am someone who ____

____ live in the countryside.

785. I am someone who might ____

____ just for fun.

786. I am someone who ____

____ homesteading.

787. I am someone who hoards ____

____.

788. I am someone who keeps ____

____ when I should throw them away.

789. I am someone who never uses ______________________________________

____.

790. I am someone who always uses _____________________________________

____.

791. I am someone who ____

____ test taker.

792. I am someone who ____

____ Rorschach test.

793. I am someone who has taken a tour of ______________________________

____.

794. I am someone who always keeps ______________________________

____ on hand.

795. I am someone who stockpiles ______________________________

because ______________________________________.

796. I am someone who ______________________________

____ funerals.

797. I am someone who ______________________________

____ weddings.

798. I am someone who ______________________________

late and ________________________________ on time.

799. I am someone who likes to chew on ______________________________

____.

800. I am someone who usually orders takeout from ______________________________

____.

801. I am someone who uses the condiment ______________________________

____ the most.

802. I am someone who ______________________________

________________________________ uses the microwave.

803. I am someone who keeps ______________________________

________________________________ next to my bed.

804. I am someone who describes their dream home as ______________________

____.

805. I am someone who ____

______________________________ when I meet a rude person.

806. I am someone who ____

______________________________________ stand-up comedy.

807. I am someone who ____

____ adopt a child.

808. I am someone who ____

__________________________________ to play an instrument.

809. I am someone who never leaves home without ______________________

____.

810. I am someone who gets good vibes from __________________________

____.

811. I am someone who gags when ________________________________

____.

812. I am someone who is out of the loop when it comes to ______________

____.

813. I am someone who ____

____ garden.

814. I am someone who ____

____ planted a tree.

815. I am someone who needs to confront ____________________

about ____________________.

816. I am someone who ____________________

____________________ good deeds.

817. I am someone who is still learning to navigate ____________________

____________________.

818. I am someone who nobody seems to ____________________

____________________.

819. I am someone who everybody seems to ____________________

____________________.

820. I am someone who my friends always come to for ____________________

____________________.

821. I am someone who can't ____________________

____________________.

822. I am someone who can ____________________

____________________.

823. I am someone who is ____________________

____________________ at lying when I do tell a lie.

824. I am someone who could convince you to ____________________

____________________.

825. I am someone who ____________________

____________________ try new things.

826. I am someone who always wonders "what if" ______________________

______________________.

827. I am someone who the glass is ______________________

______________________.

828. I am someone who thinks ______________________

______________________ is uplifting.

829. I am someone who ______________________

______________________ tears me down.

830. I am someone who ______________________

______________________ if I have no plans.

831. I am someone who ______________________

______________________ makes my life easier.

832. I am someone who ______________________

______________________ is a toxic trait I need to change.

833. I am someone who is happiest when I ______________________

______________________.

834. I am someone who needs to find out ______________________

______________________.

835. I am someone who gets sentimental when I think about ______________________

______________________.

836. I am someone who ______________________

______________________ will always be my number one goal.

837. I am someone who ______________________________

when ______________________________ got canceled.

838. I am someone who always takes pictures of ______________________________

______________________________.

839. I am someone who holds ______________________________

______________________________ in high regard.

840. I am someone who ______________________________

______________________________ makes me feel blessed.

841. I am someone who wouldn't trade ______________________________

______________________________ for anything in the world.

842. I am someone who ______________________________

______________________________ is kicking my ass right now.

843. I am someone who had buyer's remorse when I bought ______________________________

______________________________.

844. I am someone who likes my ______________________________

______________________________ fluffy.

845. I am someone who has a ______________________________

______________________________ desk.

846. I am someone who ______________________________

______________________________ makes me feel invigorated.

847. I am someone who will never forget ______________________________

because ______________________________.

848. I am someone who ___

___ was the scariest moment of my life.

849. I am someone who is patient when it comes to ___

___.

850. I am someone who would love to collaborate with ___

___.

851. I am someone who needs to learn acceptance when it comes to ___

___.

852. I am someone who needs to be more assertive with ___

___.

853. I am someone who ___

___ throw somebody under the bus (aka backstabbed) to get something I wanted.

854. I am someone who ___

generous with ___.

855. I am someone who ___

is detrimental to my ___.

856. I am someone who ___

___ hurts my dignity.

857. I am someone who lacks self-control with ___

___.

858. I am someone who has good self-control when it comes to ___

___.

859. I am someone who thinks the safety of ______________________________

______________________________ needs improvement.

860. I am someone who feels very secure about my ______________________________

______________________________.

861. I am someone who has a clear vision for ______________________________

and it looks like ______________________________.

862. I am someone who ______________________________

______________________________ gives me a sense of community.

863. I am someone who ______________________________

______________________________ knows what to do in tough situations.

864. I am someone who ______________________________

______________________________ at gift giving.

865. I am someone who goes for a walk ______________________________

______________________________.

866. I am someone who ______________________________

______________________________ unplugs from social media and devices (digital detox).

867. I am someone who ______________________________

______________________________ meditates.

868. I am someone who always calls ______________________________

______________________________ when I am in trouble.

869. I am someone who has an interesting ______________________________

______________________________.

870. I am someone who has ______________________________

______________________________ manners.

871. I am someone who would describe some of my mannerisms as ______________________________

______________________________.

872. I am someone who blushes when ______________________________

______________________________.

873. I am someone who has a complicated relationship with ______________________________

______________________________.

874. I am someone who thinks ______________________________

______________________________ shouldn't be a holiday.

875. I am someone who thinks there should be a holiday dedicated to ______________________________

______________________________.

876. I am someone who burnt a bridge when I ______________________________

______________________________.

877. I am someone who wants to learn how to play ______________________________

______________________________.

878. I am someone who if dared might ______________________________

______________________________.

879. I am someone who had to face serious consequences when I ______________________________

______________________________.

880. I am someone who could spend all day ______________________________

______________________________.

881. I am someone who sees themselves ______________________________

______________________________ in the next 5 years.

882. I am someone who thinks I am worthy of ______________________________

______________________________.

883. I am someone who sometimes self-sabotages when I ______________________________

______________________________.

884. I am someone who recently discovered a new passion for ______________________________

______________________________.

885. I am someone who is ______________________________

______________________________ pragmatic.

886. I am someone who recently added ______________________________

______________________________ to my resume.

887. I am someone who worked at ______________________________

______________________________ for my first job.

888. I am someone who learned ______________________________

from ______________________________.

889. I am someone who is currently working as ______________________________

______________________________.

890. I am someone who has failed at ______________________________

______________________________ but I'm not ready to give up.

891. I am someone who would ______________________________

______________________________ if I had unlimited time.

892. I am someone who ______________________________

______________________________ tugs at my heartstrings.

893. I am someone who never gets tired of talking about ______________________________

______________________________.

894. I am someone who considers ______________________________

______________________________ the love of my life.

895. I am someone who considers ______________________________

______________________________ the biggest mistake of my life.

896. I am someone who ______________________________

______________________________ keeps me grounded.

897. I am someone who is ______________________________

______________________________ successful.

898. I am someone who ______________________________

______________________________ irritates me.

899. I am someone who ______________________________

______________________________ calms me down.

900. I am someone who is grateful for the opportunity I was given to ______________________________

______________________________.

901. I am someone who made a wise decision when I ______________________________

______________________________.

902. I am someone who is trying to further my career by ______________________________

______________________________.

903. I am someone who ______________________________

my high school reunion because ______________________________.

904. I am someone who is thankful I get to ______________________________

______________________________.

905. I am someone who builds others up by ______________________________

______________________________.

906. I am someone who loves to go on outings to ______________________________

______________________________.

907. I am someone who was backstabbed by ______________________________

______________________________.

908. I am someone who has a coworker that ______________________________

______________________________.

909. I am someone who has pretended to be fine when actually I was ______________________________

______________________________.

910. I am someone who shares a special bond with ______________________________

______________________________.

911. I am someone who wants to make a pilgrimage to ______________________________

to ______________________________.

912. I am someone who never liked ______________________________

______________________________ growing up but I like it now.

913. I am someone who loves to ______________________________

______________________________ because it makes me feel like a kid again.

914. I am someone who has had to suppress my feelings of ______________________

in order to ____.

915. I am someone who has fond memories of the summer when ______________

____.

916. I am someone who will always remember the first time I ______________

____.

917. I am someone who never understood why my parents ______________

____.

918. I am someone who is always having to justify ______________

____.

919. I am someone who got caught by my parents ______________

____.

920. I am someone who caught their parents ______________

____.

921. I am someone who wants to do ______________

______________________________ different than my parents did.

922. I am someone who needs to change their perspective on ______________

because ____.

923. I am someone who hopes one day to change someone else's life by ______________

____.

924. I am someone who ______________________________

is a big deal in my life and means ______________________________.

925. I am someone who thinks the song ______________________________

______________________________ best represents me and my life.

926. I am someone who plays ______________________________

______________________________ when I want to dance or feel good.

927. I am someone who would pack ______________________________

______________________________ as my ideal picnic lunch.

928. I am someone who notices ______________________________

______________________________.

929. I am someone who has a strange habit of ______________________________

______________________________.

930. I am someone who if given the chance to be reincarnated would like to come back as

a ______________________________.

931. I am someone who still plays with ______________________________

______________________________.

932. I am someone who thinks ______________________________

is a gift and should be ______________________________.

933. I am someone who owns their own ______________________________

______________________________.

934. I am someone who wants to own ______________________________

______________________________ one day.

935. I am someone who needs to forgive myself for ______________________________

______________________________.

936. I am someone who ______________________________

______________________________ asks for what I want.

937. I am someone who doesn't like unexpected ______________________________

______________________________.

938. I am someone who ______________________________

______________________________ makes decisions based on my feelings.

939. I am someone who would do ______________________________

______________________________ if I knew I wouldn't fail.

940. I am someone who would describe my 16th birthday as ______________________________

______________________________.

941. I am someone who would describe my 18th birthday as ______________________________

______________________________.

942. I am someone who would describe my 21st birthday as ______________________________

______________________________.

943. I am someone who had my most memorable birthday for ______________________________

______________________________.

944. I am someone who describes intimacy as ______________________________

______________________________.

945. I am someone who does ______________________________

______________________________ when I flirt.

946. I am someone who does ______________________________

______________________________ when I am interested in someone.

947. I am someone who respects ______

dedication to ______.

948. I am someone who ______

______ has been weighing heavy on my mind.

949. I am someone who doesn't want to let ______

______ down.

950. I am someone who eases loved ones by ______

______ when they feel upset or in pain.

951. I am someone who ______

______ is my kryptonite.

952. I am someone who ______

can be a hindrance to my progress with ______.

953. I am someone who nurtures my mind and body by ______

______.

954. I am someone who ______

______ is an anchor in my life.

955. I am someone who ______

touches my soul and moves me in a way ______.

956. I am someone who loves to spend quiet time ______

______.

957. I am someone who can be judgmental of other people about ______

______.

958. I am someone who is still trying to acclimate to ______________________________

____.

959. I am someone who had a surreal moment when ______________________________

____.

960. I am someone who ____

____ taught me how to drive.

961. I am someone who would describe my ideal weather as ______________________

____.

962. I am someone who has noticed a reoccurring pattern of ______________________

____ in my life.

963. I am someone who can't take ____

____ seriously.

964. I am someone who ____

____ is my favorite fruit.

965. I am someone who ____

____ is my favorite vegetable.

966. I am someone who ____

____ is my favorite dessert.

967. I am someone who tops their pizza with ____________________________________

____.

968. I am someone who isn't close to my ______________________________________

____ even though they are family.

969. I am someone who feels like they are running from ____________________

____.

970. I am someone who overcame one of my biggest obstacles by ____________________

____.

971. I am someone who felt most uncomfortable when ____________________

____.

972. I am someone who would ____________________

____________________ if I had unlimited resources.

973. I am someone who denies myself ____________________

because ____.

974. I am someone who finds it hard to accept when people compliment me on __________

____.

975. I am someone who has ____________________

____________________ scavenger hunt.

976. I am someone who comes full circle ____________________

____.

977. I am someone who has experienced déjà vu when ____________________

____.

978. I am someone who is privileged to have ____________________

____.

979. I am someone who hopes to have a once-in-a-lifetime experience __________

____.

980. I am someone who ______________________________

______________________________ keeps me on my toes.

981. I am someone who defines quality time with my partner as ______________________________

______________________________.

982. I am someone who has fitness goals of ______________________________

______________________________.

983. I am someone who feels bad how ______________________________

______________________________ ended.

984. I am someone who understands ______________________________

is a necessary evil but wish ______________________________.

985. I am someone who has restrictions with ______________________________

______________________________.

986. I am someone who loved ______________________________

______________ when I was younger but lost touch with that part of my life.

987. I am someone who has had recent growth with ______________________________

______________________________.

988. I am someone who ______________________________

______________________________ superstitious.

989. I am someone who ______________________________

______________________________ puts me on high alert.

990. I am someone who realizes my parents were right about ______________________________

______________________________.

991. I am someone who ____________________

____________________ when I get off track.

992. I am someone who ____________________

____________________ when I feel out of balance.

993. I am someone who ____________________

is the favorite part of my day because ____________________.

994. I am someone who wishes they could go back and do ____________________

____________________ differently.

995. I am someone who ____________________

____________________ other people's culture.

996. I am someone who ____________________

____________________ share my culture.

997. I am someone who thinks ____________________

____________________ are real when other people think they are a myth.

998. I am someone who ____________________

____________________ college.

999. I am someone who envisions a world where ____________________

____________________.

1000. I am someone who usually snacks on ____________________

____________________ when I get the munchies.

1001. I am someone who hated ____________________

____________________ as a kid but love it now that I'm older.

1002. I am someone who wants to see ______________________________

______________________________ in concert.

1003. I am someone who ______________________________

______________________________ makes excuses.

1004. I am someone who goes to ______________________________

______________________________ when I need a shoulder to cry on.

1005. I am someone who likes to resolve conflicts by ______________________________

______________________________.

1006. I am someone who thinks the biggest threat to our planet right now is ______________________________

______________________________.

1007. I am someone who is predictable when it comes to ______________________________

______________________________.

1008. I am someone who is trying to be a good influence on ______________________________

______________________________.

1009. I am someone who has been negatively influenced by ______________________________

______________________________.

1010. I am someone who was affected negatively when my parents ______________________________

______________________________.

1011. I am someone who was affected positively when my parents ______________________________

______________________________.

1012. I am someone who ______________________________

______________________________ been to therapy.

1013. I am someone who is considering ending a friendship with ______________________

because ____.

1014. I am someone who needs to incorporate more ______________________________

______________________________ in my life to be more well-rounded.

1015. I am someone who can't tolerate ______________________________

______________________________ in any relationship.

1016. I am someone who believes music has the power to ______________________

____.

1017. I am someone who ______________________________

______________________________ is the best way to win my heart.

1018. I am someone who ______________________________

______________________________ left a lasting impression on.

1019. I am someone who feels ______________________________

when I write about ______________________________.

1020. I am someone who is considering another hobby and is interested in __________

____.

1021. I am someone who would never own a ______________________________

____.

1022. I am someone who hopes to inherit ______________________________

____.

1023. I am someone who is ______________________________

relationships and ______________________________ single.

1024. I am someone who loves ______________________________

______________________________ where I live.

1025. I am someone who thinks horoscopes are ______________________________

______________________________.

1026. I am someone who knows a random interesting fact about ______________________________

______________________________.

1027. I am someone who write about ______________________________

______________________________ if I were to put to put a message in a bottle.

1028. I am someone who has unrealistic expectations about ______________________________

______________________________.

1029. I am someone who feels society puts too much pressure on us about ______________________________

______________________________.

1030. I am someone who thinks I put too much pressure on myself when it comes to ______________________________

______________________________.

1031. I am someone who thinks my family puts too much pressure on me when it comes to

______________________________.

1032. I am someone who is genuinely ______________________________

______________________________.

1033. I am someone who thinks my best friend would describe me as ______________________________

______________________________.

1034. I am someone who others might say was addicted to ______________________________

______________________________.

1035. I am someone who has learned ______________________________

from ______________________________ culture.

1036. I am someone who has a favorite teacher named ______________________________

______________________________.

1037. I am someone who thinks ______________________________

______________________________ the elderly.

1038. I am someone who tried ______________________________

______________________________ and instantly regretted it.

1039. I am someone who thinks wild animals are ______________________________

and my favorite is ______________________________.

1040. I am someone who wants to leave a legacy of ______________________________

______________________________.

1041. I am someone who needs to surrender control of ______________________________

______________________________.

1042. I am someone who motivates others by ______________________________

______________________________.

1043. I am someone who ______________________________

______________________________ helps me reach my full potential.

1044. I am someone who wants to explore new cuisine, starting with ______________________________

______________________________.

1045. I am someone who has an interest in helping others ______________________________

______________________________.

1046. I am someone who thinks a person's integrity ______________________________

____.

1047. I am someone who would describe my integrity as ______________________________

____.

1048. I am someone who is ______________________________

____ empathy.

1049. I am someone who wants to make a positive impact on the world by ______________________________

____.

1050. I am someone who is not flexible when it comes to ______________________________

____.

1051. I am someone who is flexible with ______________________________

____.

1052. I am someone who continues to improve themselves by ______________________________

____.

1053. I am someone who has an idea about ______________________________

____ that I feel is innovative.

1054. I am someone who ______________________________

____ sustainable.

1055. I am someone who adapts well to ______________________________

____.

1056. I am someone who doesn't adapt well to ______________________________

____.

1057. I am someone who is hoping to expand my ______________________________

______________________________.

1058. I am someone who learned ______________________________

______________________________ about myself recently through self-reflection.

1059. I am someone who had the honor of ______________________________

______________________________.

1060. I am someone who feels protective over ______________________________

______________________________.

1061. I am someone who thinks the best compliment I ever received was ______________________________

______________________________.

1062. I am someone who thinks the worst insult I've ever received was ______________________________

______________________________.

1063. I am someone who has a family notorious for ______________________________

______________________________.

1064. I am someone who ______________________________

______________________________ was the worst thing I ever did.

1065. I am someone who ______________________________

______________________________ was the best thing I ever did.

1066. I am someone who listens to my heart ______________________________

and my head ______________________________.

1067. I am someone who wants to be introduced to ______________________________

______________________________.

1068. I am someone who goes out of their way to ______________________________________.

1069. I am someone who made a life changing decision when ______________________________________.

1070. I am someone who would describe their journey as ______________________________________.

1071. I am someone who wants to be included in ______________________________________.

1072. I am someone who describes life as ______________________________________.

1073. I am someone who tested my endurance and physical limits when ______________________________________.

1074. I am someone who felt like an underdog when ______________________________________.

1075. I am someone who is resentful of ______________________________________.

1076. I am someone who falls in love ______________________________________.

1077. I am someone who tries not to be envious of ______________________________________.

1078. I am someone who learned the hardest lesson about trust from ______________________________________.

1079. I am someone who doesn't want to settle for ______________________________

____.

1080. I am someone who regrets not taking an opportunity to ______________________

____.

1081. I am someone who wants to be more present ______________________________

____.

1082. I am someone who wants to think of the future as an opportunity to __________

____.

1083. I am someone who wants to make amends for ______________________________

____.

1084. I am someone who thinks date nights are ________________________________

____.

1085. I am someone who thinks group dates are ________________________________

____.

1086. I am someone who thinks dating sites/apps are ____________________________

____.

1087. I am someone who had the best date of my life when ______________________

____.

1088. I am someone who had the worst date of my life when _____________________

____.

1089. I am someone who had the deck stacked against them when _________________

____ but I still came out victorious.

1090. I am someone who wants ______________________________

to walk a mile in my shoes, so they can understand ______________________________.

1091. I am someone who thought their true calling was ______________________________

______________________________.

1092. I am someone who is currently putting all my energies into ______________________________

______________________________.

1093. I am someone who now thinks their purpose is ______________________________

______________________________.

1094. I am someone who ______________________________

______________________________ brings me peace.

1095. I am someone who criticizes myself for ______________________________

______________________________.

1096. I am someone who people have labeled ______________________________

______________________________ before.

1097. I am someone who felt like a punching bag when ______________________________

______________________________.

1098. I am someone who every time it feels like I'm getting closer to ______________________________

______________________________ it slips through my fingers.

1099. I am someone who wants to create a new tradition of ______________________________

______________________________ with my own family.

1100. I am someone who would never trade ______________________________

for ______________________________.

1101. I am someone who thinks physical attractiveness is ______________________________

______________________________ than a person's personality.

1102. I am someone who had to face my own prejudice about ______________________________

______________________________.

1103. I am someone who came to a crossroads when ______________________________

______________________________.

1104. I am someone who always brags about ______________________________

______________________________.

1105. I am someone who ______________________________

______________________________ has felt like a barrier to my progress at times.

1106. I am someone who felt like they were living in a dream when ______________________________

______________________________.

1107. I am someone who 5 years ago was the kind of person who would ______________________________

______________________________ but now I'm different.

1108. I am someone who looks to ______________________________

______________________________ for leadership.

1109. I am someone who has tried to hide or disguise ______________________________

______________________________ before.

1110. I am someone who recently changed ______________________________

______________________________ and I am still getting used to it.

1111. I am someone who thinks ______________________________ feels like a game of chess

and I'm one wrong move away from ______________________________.

1112. I am someone who tried to force myself to ______

but then realized ______.

1113. I am someone who betrayed ______

and felt ______.

1114. I am someone who wants to see ______

______ when I look in the mirror.

1115. I am someone who stopped talking to ______

when ______ happened.

1116. I am someone who never used to ______

but now I always ______.

1117. I am someone who ______

______ believe in coincidences.

1118. I am someone who respects ______

that's why I am careful with ______.

1119. I am someone who has a weird habit of ______

when ______.

1120. I am someone who would do ______

______ differently than my parents did when raising my children.

1121. I am someone who appreciates that my parents ______

______ as I grew up.

1122. I am someone who knows when it's time to ______

______.

1123. I am someone who just finished working on ______________________________

____.

1124. I am someone who has a hard time keeping my ______________________________

____ clean.

1125. I am someone who can never keep my ______________________________

____ organized.

1126. I am someone who would never settle for ______________________________

____.

1127. I am someone who feels like I shortchanged myself when ______________________________

____.

1128. I am someone who needs to stop comparing myself to ______________________________

____.

1129. I am someone who needs to be more thankful for ______________________________

____.

1130. I am someone who needs to appreciate my capabilities more, specifically my __________

____.

1131. I am someone who needs to recognize ______________________________

____ is a gift.

1132. I am someone who ______________________________

chooses the path of least resistance because ______________________________.

1133. I am someone who's separating ______________________________ from

______________________________ because ______________________________.

1134. I am someone who wants to be better able to ______________________________

____.

1135. I am someone who thinks ______________________________________

____ is missing in my life.

1136. I am someone who finds it hard to get out of bed sometimes, but then I __________

____.

1117. I am someone who ____

____ the supernatural.

1138. I am someone who has felt the presence of ___________________________

____ before.

1139. I am someone who ____

____ podcast/s.

1140. I am someone who wishes life had a manual/instruction for ____________________

____.

1141. I am someone who had a previous mission in life that was ____________________

but now it's ____.

1142. I am someone who is starting to put themselves first by ____________________

____.

1143. I am someone who ____

impacted and changed me in a way that ___________________________________.

1144. I am someone who usually wakes up feeling _________________________________

____.

1145. I am someone who the song ______________________________

makes me feel nostalgic of ______________________________.

1146. I am someone who the song ______________________________

makes me feel reflective because ______________________________.

1147. I am someone who the song ______________________________

makes me feel emotional because ______________________________.

1148. I am someone who the song ______________________________

______________________________ makes me feel upbeat.

1149. I am someone who the song ______________________________

makes me feel inspired to ______________________________.

1150. I am someone who can relate to the personal struggles of ______________________________

because ______________________________.

1151. I am someone who always wants to be in control of ______________________________

______________________________.

1152. I am someone who is on track to complete ______________________________

______________________________.

1153. I am someone who is usually giving off a vibe that says ______________________________

______________________________.

1154. I am someone who feels most like myself when I ______________________________

______________________________.

1155. I am someone who people say my face sometimes looks ______________________________

______________________________.

1156. I am someone who learned ______________________________

______________________________ from failures I've had in my life.

1157. I am someone who thinks ______________________________

______________________________ is not my responsibility.

1158. I am someone who is seeking redemption for ______________________________

______________________________.

1159. I am someone who as I matured, I became more ______________________________

______________________________.

1160. I am someone who thinks conspiracy theories are ______________________________

______________________________.

1161. I am someone who ______________________________

______________________________ thinks honesty is the best policy.

1162. I am someone who wishes I didn't have doubts about ______________________________

______________________________.

1163. I am someone who thinks selfies are ______________________________

______________________________.

1164. I am someone who it would be out of character for me to ______________________________

______________________________.

1165. I am someone who feels like I have an extended family in ______________________________

______________________________.

1166. I am someone who is ______________________________

______________________________ talking about my feelings.

1167. I am someone who is trying to get to the root of ______________________________

____.

1168. I am someone who holds ____

____ near and dear to my heart.

1169. I am someone who learned ____

____ from my weaknesses.

1170. I am someone who learned ____

____ from my strength.

1171. I am someone who is still figuring out why I always ______________________

____.

1172. I am someone who defines happiness as ___________________________________

____.

1173. I am someone who defines a healthy relationship as ______________________

____.

1174. I am someone who has a bond with ______________________________________

I would describe it as ____.

1175. I am someone who has ____

____ memorized.

1176. I am someone who always feels like I'm in limbo when ______________________

____.

1177. I am someone who ____

________________ can be a hindrance to to me achieving what I want out of life.

1178. I am someone who lowered my standards when ________________________________

____.

1179. I am someone who recently acquired ________________________________

____.

1180. I am someone who ________________________________

________________________________ is a recent development in my life.

1181. I am someone who ________________________________

________________________________ makes my life easier.

1182. I am someone who ________________________________

________________________________ sometimes feels like a curse.

1183. I am someone who notices ________________________________

________________________________ in others and I sometimes wish I had it too.

1184. I am someone who ________________________________

________________________________ is my favorite cologne/perfume.

1185. I am someone who sometimes feels sorry for myself when ________________

____.

1186. I am someone who defines courage as ________________________________

____.

1187. I am someone who defines an enemy as ________________________________

____.

1188. I am someone who describes peace as ________________________________

____.

1189. I am someone who is drawn to ______________________________

______________________________ in my surroundings.

1190. I am someone who is drawn to ______________________________

______________________________ opportunities.

1191. I am someone who is drawn to physical traits like ______________________________

______________________________ in others.

1192. I am someone who is drawn to specific environments like ______________________________

______________________________.

1193. I am someone who thinks perfection is ______________________________

______________________________.

1194. I am someone who ______________________________

can be crippling for me and that's why I ______________________________.

1195. I am someone who ______________________________

______________________________ is currently going good in my life.

1196. I am someone who ______________________________

______________________________ is not going so well in my life right now.

1197. I am someone who ______________________________

feels like a magnet always pulling me to ______________________________.

1198. I am someone who ______________________________

gives me knots in my ______________________________.

1199. I am someone who talking about ______________________________

makes me feel ______________________________.

1200. I am someone who always has the song ____________________

____________________ on my playlist.

1201. I am someone who avoids the song ____________________

____________________ because it's too painful.

1202. I am someone who is ____________________

____________________ at sketching/drawing.

1203. I am someone who is ____________________

____________________ at painting.

1204. I am someone who has ____________________

____________________ on their wish list.

1205. I am someone who doesn't understand the popularity or appeal of ____________________

____________________.

1206. I am someone who had an encounter with a bully when ____________________

____________________.

1207. I am someone who thinks ____________________

____________________ feels like a boomerang and always comes back to me.

1208. I am someone who tries to live by the commandment ____________________

____________________.

1209. I am someone who ____________________

____________________ is a law where I live that I respect.

1210. I am someone who had an unforgettable outing with my family when ____________________

____________________.

1211. I am someone who knowing what I know now would do ______________________

____ differently.

1212. I am someone who thinks other people's opinions are ______________________

____.

1213. I am someone who finally had enough of ______________________

____.

1214. I am someone who had to outgrow ______________________

in order to ____.

1215. I am someone who would go back in time so I could visit ______________________

____.

1216. I am someone who wants to relive ______________________

____.

1217. I am someone who cherishes the time when my grandparents ______________________

____.

1218. I am someone who ______________________

______________________ could be the best thing to happen to me today.

1219. I am someone who ______________________

free thinker and ______________________ herd mentality.

1220. I am someone who needs to stop complaining about ______________________

and take action to ____.

1221. I am someone who needs to stop ______________________

and be more grateful I have ____.

1222. I am someone who received a meaningful gift from ______________________________

____.

1223. I am someone who would describe my tech abilities as ______________________________

____.

1224. I am someone who ____

represents my ancestors and I want to ______________________________.

1225. I am someone who tell my children a story about the time when ______________________

____.

1226. I am someone who would read my favorite nursery rhyme ______________________

______________________________ to my kids as they grew up.

1227. I am someone who would watch and share my favorite childhood cartoon ____________

______________________________ with my kids.

1228. I am someone who will pass down my family's recipe of ______________________

______________________________ to my children and future generations.

1229. I am someone who thinks ____

______________________________ is an underrated family value.

1230. I am someone who thinks ____

______________________ is an underrated family activity and should be done more.

1231. I am someone who ____

______________________ is my preferred way to spend bonding time with my family.

1232. I am someone who checks in with themselves by ______________________________

____.

1233. I am someone who would describe my ego as ____________________

____________________.

1234. I am someone who would describe my temper as ____________________

____________________.

1235. I am someone who would describe my disposition as ____________________

____________________.

1236. I am someone who would describe my ideology as ____________________

____________________.

1237. I am someone who is ____________________

__________ at reading a room and understanding what people are feeling.

1238. I am someone who was heroic when ____________________

____________________.

1239. I am someone who was going through a phase when I ____________________

____________________.

1240. I am someone who tried to find themselves by ____________________

____________________.

1241. I am someone who sometimes intimidates others when ____________________

____________________.

1242. I am someone who needs to stop ____________________

____________________ other people.

1243. I am someone who needs to listen to ____________________

____________________ more.

1244. I am someone who recently had my eyes opened to ______________________________

____.

1245. I am someone who recently learned how to ______________________________

____.

1246. I am someone who loves reminiscing about ______________________________

____.

1247. I am someone who used to not appreciate ______________________________

but then____.

1248. I am someone who was reckless with ______________________________

but changed when ____.

1249. I am someone who used to be ashamed of ______________________________

but then I realized ____.

1250. I am someone who can't believe I used to ______________________________

____.

1251. I am someone who can honestly say I am in a better place now than ____________

because of ____.

1252. I am someone who describes the public me as ______________________________

____.

1253. I am someone who describes the private me as ______________________________

____.

1254. I am someone who put ____

on the back burner until ____.

1255. I am someone who the quickest way to make me laugh is ______________________________

____.

1256. I am someone who the quickest way to win my heart is ______________________________

____.

1257. I am someone who never gets tired of talking about ______________________________

____.

1258. I am someone who never gets tired of thinking about ______________________________

____.

1259. I am someone who never gets tired of hanging around ______________________________

____.

1260. I am someone who the last lie I told was ______________________________

____.

1261. I am someone who the last argument I had was with ______________________________

about ____.

1262. I am someone who the last goal I made was ______________________________

____.

1263. I am someone who the last nice thing I did for myself was ______________________________

____.

1264. I am someone who the last selfless act I did was ______________________________

____.

1265. I am someone who wishes people could see me as ______________________________

____.

1266. I am someone who wishes I was more laid back with ______________________________

____.

1267. I am someone who would add ______________________________________

______________________________________ to a new vision board I create.

1268. I am someone who the benefits of my size and height are ______________________

____.

1269. I am someone who the benefits of my personality are __________________________

____.

1270. I am someone who the benefits of my abilities are ____________________________

____.

1271. I am someone who the benefits of being myself are ___________________________

____.

1272. I am someone who would love to have the superpower of ______________________

____.

1273. I am someone who would hate to have the superpower of ______________________

____.

1274. I am someone who thinks the ideal superpower yet to be designed would be ________

____.

1275. I am someone who would love to learn the language __________________________

so I can ____.

1276. I am someone who if my life was a movie I would want it directed by ____________

____.

1277. I am someone who ______________________________

______________________________ is my biggest cheerleader.

1278. I am someone who ______________________________

______________________________ is my toughest critic.

1279. I am someone who ______________________________

______________________________ is my number one hater.

1280. I am someone who ______________________________

______________________________ is my emergency contact.

1281. I am someone who knows ______________________________

______________________________ tells me the truth no matter how hard it is.

1282. I am someone who thinks ______________________________

______________________________ has an ideal life.

1283. I am someone who thinks I have no more room in my life for ______________________________

______________________________.

1284. I am someone who has an inner child that always wants to ______________________________

______________________________.

1285. I am someone who has an inner child that wants to tell my adult self that ______________________________

______________________________.

1286. I am someone who wants to comfort my inner child by reminding myself ______________________________

______________________________.

1287. I am someone who didn't get ______________________________

as a child and that's why I ______________________________.

1288. I am someone who the hardest discipline for me to follow is ____________________

____.

1289. I am someone who hardest situation to get out of was ____________________

____.

1290. I am someone who the hardest relationship I had was with ____________________

because ____.

1291. I am someone who the hardest truth I had to learn was ____________________

____.

1292. I am someone who ____

____ when I want attention.

1293. I am someone who describes stability as ____________________

____.

1294. I am someone who describes security as ____________________

____.

1295. I am someone who describes respect as ____________________

____.

1296. I am someone who describes integrity as ____________________

____.

1297. I am someone who describes loyalty as ____________________

____.

1298. I am someone who describes betrayal as ____________________

____.

1299. I am someone who the biggest influence (not a person) that shaped my life was ______

______.

1300. I am someone who is thinking about a new challenge that involves ______

______.

1301. I am someone who is thinking about a new adventure that will include ______

______.

1302. I am someone who is thinking about a new passion that will ______

______.

1303. I am someone who wants to add new things to my life such as ______

______.

1304. I am someone who wants the next chapter of my life to look like ______

______.

1305. I am someone who wants the next part of my story to include ______

______.

1306. I am someone who wants my future to be filled with ______

______.

1307. I am someone who wants to revisit unresolved ______

______.

1308. I am someone who wants to confront buried fears that are unrealized like ______

______.

1309. I am someone who wants to face my greatest phobia of ______

by ______.

1310. I am someone who admires ______________________________
______________________________ about myself.

1311. I am someone who admires ______________________________
______________________________ ability to adapt.

1312. I am someone who has had unexplained occurrences in my life like ______________________________
______________________________.

1313. I am someone who handles the unexpected ______________________________
______________________________.

1314. I am someone who would handle blackmail by ______________________________
______________________________.

1315. I am someone who would handle corruption by ______________________________
______________________________.

1316. I am someone who would handle insurmountable odds by ______________________________
______________________________.

1317. I am someone who would handle an attack on my character by ______________________________
______________________________.

1318. I am someone who ______________________________
______________________________ marry royalty.

1319. I am someone who ______________________________
______________________________ marry a celebrity.

1320. I am someone who ______________________________
______________________________ marry my long-term best friend.

1321. I am someone who ______________________

______________________ marry a person several years younger than me.

1322. I am someone who ______________________

______________________ date one of my teachers.

1323. I am someone who ______________________

______________________date one of my friend's ex's.

1324. I am someone who ______________________

______________________ date someone one of my siblings dated.

1325. I am someone who ______________________

______________________ date someone I already dated and broke up with.

1326. I am someone who ______________________

______________________ date one of my siblings' closest friends.

1327. I am someone who ______________________

______________________ in love at first sight.

1328. I am someone who ______________________

______________________ fairytale endings.

1329. I am someone who ______________________

______________________ opposites attract.

1330. I am someone who ______________________

______________________ practice makes perfect.

1331. I am someone who ______________________

cost me an arm and a leg because ______________________.

1332. I am someone who has cut corners when I ____

____.

1333. I am someone who had my back against the wall when ____________________________

and it forced me to ____.

1334. I am someone who escaped ____

by the skin of my teeth because ____.

1335. I am someone who thinks ____

____ is easier said than done.

1336. I am someone who was up a creek without a paddle when I ____________________________

____.

1337. I am someone who felt like a fish out of water when ____________________________

____.

1338. I am someone who will always go the extra mile for ____________________________

____.

1339. I am someone who needs to step their game up when it comes to ____________________________

____.

1340. I am someone who threw caution to the wind when I ____________________________

____.

1341. I am someone who once bit off more than I could chew when I ____________________________

____.

1342. I am someone who had to go back to the drawing board when ____________________________

____.

1343. I am someone who has been through thick and thin with ______________________________

____.

1344. I am someone who loves to ______________________________

once in a blue moon when I am feeling ______________________________.

1345. I am someone who one time in school got a slap on the wrist for ______________________________

____.

1346. I am someone who got caught in the heat of the moment when ______________________________

and it resulted in ______________________________.

1347. I am someone who had a rumor spread like wildfire about me that was ______________________________

____.

1348. I am someone who took a backseat to ______________________________

so progress could be made with ______________________________.

1349. I am someone who accidentally rocked the boat by ______________________________

and now ______________________________.

1350. I am someone who is trying to play my cards right so I can ______________________________

____.

1351. I am someone who has been told I was in a league of my own when it comes to ______________________________

____.

1352. I am someone who has put my blood, sweat and tears into ______________________________

____.

1353. I am someone who had the most memorable coming of age moment when ______________________________

____.

1354. I am someone who never in a million years thought ______________________________

____.

1355. I am someone who has been thinking there's no time like the present for me to ________

____.

1356. I am someone who thinks the ship may have sailed on my opportunity for ____________

____.

1357. I am someone who has an axe to grind with ___________________________________

____.

1358. I am someone who would compare their life to the famous painting _______________

______________________ because ____.

1359. I am someone who has recently been introduced to _____________________________

and I ____.

1360. I am someone who ____

brings out my artistic side and allows me to ____________________________________.

1361. I am someone who always strategizes when I _________________________________

____.

1362. I am someone who is currently on a roll with _________________________________

____.

1363. I am someone who ____

gets me pumped up and allows me to ____.

1364. I am someone who has a specific checklist for _________________________________

because I want to make sure ____.

1365. I am someone who could do ______________________________

______________________________ blindfolded.

1366. I am someone who was between a rock and a hard place when I had to ______________

______________________________.

1367. I am someone who thinks ______________________________

is a gift but sometimes feels like a curse because ______________________________.

1368. I am someone who had a hard time recovering from ______________________________

______________________________.

1369. I am someone who went through a drastic time when ______________________________

and it called for desperate measures like ______________________________.

1370. I am someone who could use a good cleansing of my ______________________________

______________________________.

1371. I am someone who had to level the playing field when I ______________________________

so I decided to ______________________________.

1372. I am someone who succumbed to peer pressure when I ______________________________

______________________________.

1373. I am someone who recognizes that I am valuable because ______________________________

______________________________.

1374. I am someone who many of my friends love ______________________________

______________________________ but it's just not my cup of tea.

1375. I am someone who would rate my mental fitness as ______________________________

______________________________.

1376. I am someone who thinks ______

______ will always be worth the risk.

1377. I am someone who wishes I could ______

______ for an entire day undisturbed.

1378. I am someone who out of all my friends is most likely to ______

______.

1379. I am someone who out of all my friends is least likely to ______

______.

1380. I am someone who had something so strange happen when ______

______ people don't believe me.

1381. I am someone who knows myself on a scale of 1-10 ______

______.

1382. I am someone who knows my best friend on a scale of 1-10 ______

______.

1383. I am someone who knows my significant other on a scale of 1-10 ______

______.

1384. I am someone who ______

______ present in my personal relationships.

1385. I am someone who would like people to recognize ______

______ in me more.

1386. I am someone who thinks a better version of myself would look like ______

______.

1387. I am someone who used to hide ______________________________

______________________________ from my parents.

1388. I am someone who used to hide ______________________________

______________________________ from my friends.

1389. I am someone who used to have big disagreements with my parents over ______________

______________________________.

1390. I am someone who had the biggest disagreement with my closest friend over ______________

______________________________.

1391. I am someone who asserts myself by ______________________________

______________________________.

1392. I am someone who reassures myself by ______________________________

______________________________.

1393. I am someone who ______________________________

______________________________ random hookups.

1394. I am someone who ______________________________

______________________________ serious relationships.

1395. I am someone who ______________________________

______________________________ best friends in my life.

1396. I am someone who ______________________________

______________________________ cheated in a relationship.

1397. I am someone who ______________________________

______________________________ cheated on a test.

1398. I am someone who pays attention to ______________________________

______________________________.

1399. I am someone who the little details of ______________________________

______________________________ are important to me.

1400. I am someone who has my hands full with ______________________________

______________________________.

1401. I am someone who got cold feet when it came to ______________________________

______________________________.

1402. I am someone who gets butterflies when ______________________________

______________________________.

1403. I am someone who sleeps ______________________________

______________________________.

1404. I am someone who thought ______________________________

seemed like a long shot but then ______________________________.

1405. I am someone who went out on a limb for ______________________________

______________________________.

1406. I am someone who is ______________________________ frugal and

______________________________ extravagant.

1407. I am someone who does ______________________________

______________________________ when I flirt.

1408. I am someone who had the time of my life when ______________________________

______________________________.

1409. I am someone who was trying to outrun ________________

but now I am ________________.

1410. I am someone who thinks ________________

________________ is better with a friend.

1411. I am someone who thinks ________________

________________ should only be done with family.

1412. I am someone who thinks ________________

________________ is better with someone you love.

1413. I am someone who thinks trust is lost when ________________

________________.

1414. I am someone who thinks communication breaks down when ________________

________________.

1415. I am someone who thinks friends should never ________________

________________.

1416. I am someone who parents should never ________________

________________ to their children.

1417. I am someone who thinks cash is ________________

________________.

1418. I am someone who thinks credit cards are ________________

________________.

1419. I am someone who has zero time for people who are ________________

________________.

1420. I am someone who thinks celebrities that have a platform should not use it to ________________________________.

1421. I am someone who thinks celebrities that have a platform should use it for ________________________________.

1422. I am someone who ________________________________ impacted by someone with an addiction.

1423. I am someone who believes ________________________________ should be earned and not given to anyone.

1424. I am someone who loves to ________________________________ when I take a shower or bath.

1425. I am someone who always ________________________________ when I get my paycheck.

1426. I am someone who believes meaningful experiences can ________________________________.

1427. I am someone who loves the designer brand ________________________________.

1428. I am someone who ________________________________ winds me up.

1429. I am someone who ________________________________ winds me down.

1430. I am someone who hopes my children inherit my ________________________________.

1431. I am someone who ______________________________

______________________________ street smarts.

1432. I am someone who ______________________________

is not in my big picture and I need to decide how to ______________.

1433. I am someone who used to be afraid of ______________________

but then ______________________________.

1434. I am someone who ______________________________

______________________________ popular.

1435. I am someone who is most comfortable around ______________

______________________________.

1436. I am someone who if I'm quiet it usually means ______________

______________________________.

1437. I am someone who ______________________________

______________________________ friend zone.

1438. I am someone who ______________________________

______________________________ be friends with an ex.

1439. I am someone who ______________________________

______________________________ people keeping secrets from me.

1440. I am someone who finds it hard to keep a straight face when ______________

______________________________.

1441. I am someone who has allowed people to ______________________

before but now I am ______________________________.

1442. I am someone who can be overly cautious about ______________________

____.

1443. I am someone who hates when people think I am ______________________

____.

1444. I am someone who ____

____ always gives me a headache.

1445. I am someone who ____

____ is a pain in my ass.

1446. I am someone who ____

____ makes my stomach hurt.

1447. I am someone who has suffered from ______________________________

____.

1448. I am someone who felt like a doormat before when __________________

____.

1449. I am someone who was triumphant when ___________________________

____.

1450. I am someone who thinks ____

____________________________________ is essential for good mental health.

1451. I am someone who thinks everyone should _________________________

____ at least once in their lives.

1452. I am someone who thinks ____

___________________________________ is essential for good physical health.

1453. I am someone who thinks ______________________________

______________________________ is the most influential mogul of this century.

1454. I am someone who thinks the most versatile actor of this century is ______________

______________________________.

1455. I am someone who thinks the most inspirational artist of all time is ______________

______________________________.

1456. I am someone who ______________________________

______________________________ date someone I worked with.

1457. I am someone who ______________________________

______________________________ date my boss.

1458. I am someone who never skips ______________________________

______________________________.

1459. I am someone who ______________________________

______________________________ more than once a day.

1460. I am someone who ______________________________

______________________________ when I want to channel nervous energy.

1461. I am someone who always asks permission before I ______________________________

______________________________.

1462. I am someone who hates attending ______________________________

______________________________.

1463. I am someone who loves attending ______________________________

______________________________.

1464. I am someone who thinks the most unattractive people are ones who ______________________

____.

1465. I am someone who thinks ____

______________________________ are becoming more and more irrelevant.

1466. I am someone who thinks ____

______________________________________ will never go out of style.

1467. I am someone who ____

__________ date/marry someone with a different faith or religion other than mine.

1468. I am someone who ____

____________________________ date/marry someone with a criminal record.

1469. I am someone who ____

_______________________________________ long-distance relationships.

1470. I am someone who ____

____ problem solving.

1471. I am someone who thinks wisdom comes from _______________________________

____.

1472. I am someone who lets ____

____ guide me.

1473. I am someone who ____

____ pros and cons.

1474. I am someone who ____

____ consequences.

1475. I am someone who ______________________________

______________________________ brings out the worst in me.

1476. I am someone who needs to learn how to say no to ______________________________

______________________________.

1477. I am someone who loves ______________________________

______________________________ about life.

1478. I am someone who if there were no laws I would probably ______________________________

______________________________.

1479. I am someone who will always pick ______________________________

______________________________ out of a vending machine.

1480. I am someone who ______________________________

______________________________ humble.

1481. I am someone who will never change ______________________________

______________________________ about myself.

1482. I am someone who ______________________________

______________________________ was the most painful thing I've been through.

1483. I am someone who still needs closure from ______________________________

______________________________.

1484. I am someone who ______________________________ takeout/fast food

______________________________ cooking at home.

1485. I am someone who ______________________________

______________________________ sign language.

1486. I am someone who is ______________________________

______________________________ attracted to something if I know it's forbidden.

1487. I am someone who has an unusual ______________________________

______________________________.

1488. I am someone who want my ghost to haunt ______________________________

______________________________.

1489. I am someone who ______________________________

______________________________ and that would rank as the wildest thing I've ever done so far.

1490. I am someone who refused to ______________________________

______________________________ as a child but now I do it all the time.

1491. I am someone who never would have thought______________________________

would happen, but now I believe ______________________________.

1492. I am someone who given the chance to have dinner with someone no longer alive, it

would be ______________________________.

1493. I am someone who ______________________________

______________________________ been naked in public.

1494. I am someone who thinks the best way to break up with someone is by ______________

______________________________.

1495. I am someone who would never work in ______________________________

______________________________ industry.

1496. I am someone who wants to be closer to ______________________________

______________________________.

1497. I am someone who tried to runaway from ______________________________

____.

1498. I am someone who if I became famous, would handle it ______________________

____.

1499. I am someone who ____

____ when I dislike someone.

1500. I am someone who ____

____ when I begin liking someone.

1501. I am someone who often blames _____________________________________

____ for my problems.

1502. I am someone who has pretended to ____________________________________

so I could ____.

1503. I am someone who thinks there should be a statue of __________________________

____.

1504. I am someone who wants ____

______________________ to prepare a multiple course tasting menu for me.

1505. I am someone who is just beginning to understand my __________________________

____.

1506. I am someone who knows better than to __________________________________

____ to my parents.

1507. I am someone who would never _____________________________________

____ my family.

1508. I am someone who has been known to yell out ______________________________

when ____.

1509. I am someone who wants the people around me to feel ____________________

____.

1510. I am someone who ______________________________________

people person but ______________________________________.

1511. I am someone who always wants my birthday cake flavor to be ______________

____.

1512. I am someone who loves ______________________________________

______________________ ice cream and will say it's my favorite flavor.

1513. I am someone who will never celebrate ______________________________

____.

1514. I am someone who thinks ______________________________________

______________________________ makes life more bearable.

1515. I am someone who thinks ______________________________________

__________________ adds beauty to the everyday mundane parts of life.

1516. I am someone who ______________________________________

______________ when I feel stagnant, or things get too cloudy or unclear.

1517. I am someone who got complacent when ______________________________

____.

1518. I am someone who ______________________________________

______________________________ is a way to gain my trust.

1519. I am someone who is always questioning ______________________________

____.

1520. I am someone who feels uncertain about ______________________________

____.

1521. I am someone who first felt like an adult when ______________________________

____.

1522. I am someone who has ______________________________

____ in the last 24 hours.

1523. I am someone who had the hardest job/task of my life when ______________________________

____.

1524. I am someone who hates the photo of myself that ______________________________

____.

1525. I am someone who ______________________________

____ read a map.

1526. I am someone who knows random trivia such as ______________________________

____.

1527. I am someone who given the chance to share something about myself with the world, I would share ______________________________.

1528. I am someone who hesitates when ______________________________

____.

1529. I am someone who is very particular when it comes to ______________________________

____.

1530. I am someone who can be rebellious when ______________________________

____.

1531. I am someone who ____

______________ when I am by myself and I would never do it in front of someone.

1532. I am someone who had my longest romantic relationship with ____________

____.

1533. I am someone who had my shortest romantic relationship with ____________

____.

1534. I am someone who got away with _______________________________

____.

1535. I am someone who got caught ___________________________________

____.

1536. I am someone who was given an ultimatum _________________________

____.

1537. I am someone who thinks marijuana is ____________________________

____.

1538. I am someone who has been experimental with _____________________

____.

1539. I am someone who ____

candles, specifically ____ scent.

1540. I am someone who would describe my intelligence as _______________

____.

1541. I am someone who thinks the best part of my job is ______________________________

____.

1542. I am someone who thinks the hardest part of my job is ______________________________

____.

1543. I am someone who when people first meet me they usually ______________________________

____.

1544. I am someone who thinks they way I dress says ______________________________

____.

1545. I am someone who has a platonic relationship with ______________________________

______________________________ but I have thought about taking it further.

1546. I am someone who looked up to ______________________________

______________________________ as my role model.

1547. I am someone who would buy as much as I could of ______________________________

______________________________ if it was going to be discontinued.

1548. I am someone who thinks the most helpful subject I took in school was ______________

____.

1549. I am someone who thinks the most useless subject I took in school was ______________

____.

1550. I am someone who has a blood type of ______________________________

____.

1551. I am someone who ______________________________

______________________________ donates/donated blood.

1552. I am someone who thinks ______________________________

______________________________ negatively impacts my life.

1553. I am someone who likes ______________________________

______________________________ as foreplay.

1554. I am someone who ______________________________

______________________________ is the most scandalous thing I've done.

1555. I am someone who could fall into the stereotype of ______________________________

______________________________.

1556. I am someone who thinks a reality TV show about my life should be called ______________________________

______________________________.

1557. I am someone who ______________________________

______________________________ yoga.

1558. I am someone who ______________________________

______________________________ keeps me going.

1559. I am someone who say ______________________________

______________________________ if you ask me for relationship advice.

1560. I am someone who loves the month of ______________________________

______________________________.

1561. I am someone who has a certificate for ______________________________

______________________________.

1562. I am someone who ______________________________

______________________________ survival skills.

1563. I am someone who participated in ______________________________

______________________________ while in school.

1564. I am someone who was a member of ______________________________

______________________________ in high school.

1565. I am someone who used to get picked on for ______________________________

but now I have ______________________________.

1566. I am someone who thinks the most humiliating thing that could ever happen to me

would be ______________________________.

1567. I am someone who thinks ______________________________

______ is an important part of my surroundings/environment and I will always protect it.

1568. I am someone who ______________________________

______________________________ summer camp.

1569. I am someone who hungers for ______________________________

______________________________.

1570. I am someone who used to get caught up in ______________________________

but then I became more aware of ______________________________.

1571. I am someone who always dissects ______________________________

______________________________.

1572. I am someone who ______________________________

a bet and ______________________________.

1573. I am someone who thinks ______________________________

______________________________ are the scariest animals on the planet.

1574. I am someone who love ______________________________

______________________________ to write a song about me.

1575. I am someone who thinks Amazon is ______________________________

______________________________.

1576. I am someone who thinks ______________________________

______________________________ will change the future of the world for good.

1577. I am someone who thinks ______________________________

______________________________ will impact the future of the world negatively.

1578. I am someone who thinks ______________________________

______________________________ needs to be the next invention.

1579. I am someone who ______________________________

is impacting families negatively because ______________________________.

1580. I am someone who thinks ______________________________

______________________________ will be the newest popular sport of the future.

1581. I am someone who thinks people will get tired of ______________________________

______________________________ and it will lose popularity and become nonexistent.

1582. I am someone who thinks movie theaters are ______________________________

______________________________.

1583. I am someone who thinks bowling alleys are ______________________________

______________________________.

1584. I am someone who thinks arcades are ______________________________

______________________________.

1585. I am someone who would describe my inner warrior as ______________________

____.

1586. I am someone who can tap into ______________________________

______________________________ when I need self motivation.

1587. I am someone who wouldn't mind being stuck at the age of ______________

______________________________________ forever.

1588. I am someone who would be the perfect person to appear in a commercial featuring

____.

1589. I am someone who wishes I had never met ______________________________

____.

1590. I am someone who thinks ______________________________________

______________________ may have been the one that got away.

1591. I am someone who can be charming when I ______________________________

____.

1592. I am someone who got my driver's license when I was ______________________

____.

1593. I am someone who got my first car when I was ______________________________

____.

1594. I am someone who drove a ______________________________________

______________________________________ for my first car.

1595. I am someone who thinks casinos are ______________________________

____.

1596. I am someone who thinks the Olympics are ______________________________

______________________________.

1597. I am someone who would title the next chapter of my life as ______________________________

______________________________.

1598. I am someone who would title the current chapter of my life as ______________________________

______________________________.

1599. I am someone who would title the previous chapter of my life as ______________________________

______________________________.

1600. I am someone who keeps ______________________________

______________________________ under my bed.

1601. I am someone who wants to ______________________________

______________________________ but I don't have the money for it.

1602. I am someone who is waiting for another chance to ______________________________

______________________________.

1603. I am someone who thinks fast food chains are ______________________________

______________________________.

1604. I am someone who would describe their eating habits as ______________________________

______________________________.

1605. I am someone who needs to say "yes" to more ______________________________

______________________________.

1606. I am someone who if I was Dorothy and was thrown into OZ, I would ______________________________

______________________________.

1607. I am someone who wants my tombstone to read ______________________________

____.

1608. I am someone who if another pandemic hit again, I would ____________________

____.

1609. I am someone who wants to ____

but I am afraid of the consequences that would ____________________________.

1610. I am someone who recognizes that life is a ______________________________

and there will be ____________________ and ____________________.

1611. I am someone who thinks ____

______________________________ is worth fighting for no matter what.

1612. I am someone who would love to learn how to make my own ________________

______________________________ so I don't have to buy it anymore.

1613. I am someone who ____

____ detention in school.

1614. I am someone who thinks the worst punishment my parents ever gave me was ______

____.

1615. I am someone who thinks the best reward my parents ever gave me was ________

____.

1616. I am someone who feels like I lose a piece of myself when ____________________

____.

1617. I am someone who ____

________________ makes me feel powerful and gives me a take charge mentality.

1618. I am someone who thinks true crime documentaries and podcasts ______________________________
____.

1619. I am someone who ____
____ remakes of classic movies.

1620. I am someone who ____
____ nature documentaries.

1621. I am someone who thinks ____
____ is the best voiceover actor.

1622. I am someone who thinks privacy in today's world is ______________________________
____.

1623. I am someone who feels like crap when ____
____.

1624. I am someone who would call myself ____
____ if I ever became a rapper.

1625. I am someone who thinks you should ____
____ earlier in life.

1626. I am someone who dreams of spending my retirement era by ______________________
____.

1627. I am someone who wants their life to be a reflection of ______________________
____.

1628. I am someone who if I created a bucket list the first thing that would be on it would be
____.

1629. I am someone who realizes ______________________________

______________________________ takes time.

1630. I am someone who knows my ______________________________

______________________________.

1631. I am someone who loves celebrating ______________________________

______________________________.

1632. I am someone who wants to travel to ______________________________

______________________________.

1633. I am someone who you can always count on to ______________________________

______________________________.

1634. I am someone who is inspired by ______________________________

______________________________.

1635. I am someone who did ______________________________

______________________________ in school.

1636. I am someone who thinks ______________________________

______________________________ should be free.

1637. I am someone who has always dreamed about ______________________________

______________________________.

1638. I am someone who has a hard time ______________________________

______________________________.

1639. I am someone who gets excited about ______________________________

______________________________.

1640. I am someone who ______________________________

______________________________ when I meet new people.

1641. I am someone who wants my friends to feel ______________________________

______________________________.

1642. I am someone who laughs at myself when ______________________________

______________________________.

1643. I am someone who respects the opinions of ______________________________

______________________________.

1644. I am someone who seeks guidance from ______________________________

______________________________.

1645. I am someone who is practical when it comes to ______________________________

______________________________.

1646. I am someone who desires ______________________________

______________________________.

1647. I am someone who has been thinking about changing ______________________________

______________________________.

1648. I am someone who would never take ______________________________

______________________________ for granted.

1649. I am someone who needs attention when ______________________________

______________________________.

1650. I am someone who doesn't always show ______________________________

______________________________.

1651. I am someone who can be a handful if ______________________________

____.

1652. I am someone who goes beyond the call of duty for ____________________

____.

1653. I am someone who would relocate to ______________________________

if ____.

1654. I am someone who gets into trouble when __________________________

____.

1655. I am someone who wishes they could have a second chance ____________

____.

1656. I am someone who feels cozy when ______________________________

____.

1657. I am someone who everybody seems to ____________________________

____.

1658. I am someone who never wants to start __________________________

____.

1659. I am someone who is a champion for ______________________________

____.

1660. I am someone who won't miss an opportunity to ____________________

____.

1661. I am someone who asks myself ____________________________________

____.

1662. I am someone who thinks ______________________________

______________________________ is not real.

1663. I am someone who has bad luck when it comes to ______________________________

______________________________.

1664. I am someone who gets nervous when ______________________________

______________________________.

1665. I am someone who gets paranoid when ______________________________

______________________________.

1666. I am someone who has different hobbies, but my favorite is ______________________________

______________________________.

1667. I am someone who feels independent when ______________________________

______________________________.

1668. I am someone who is saving ______________________________

for ______________________________.

1669. I am someone who thinks you should ______________________________

______________________________ as you get older.

1670. I am someone who is skeptical about ______________________________

______________________________.

1671. I am someone who comes from a ______________________________

______________________________ family.

1672. I am someone who encourages others to ______________________________

______________________________.

1673. I am someone who thinks ______________________________

______________________________ are real.

1674. I am someone who ______________________________

______________________________ my heritage.

1675. I am someone who ______________________________

______________________________ under pressure.

1676. I am someone who wants to give back to ______________________________

______________________________.

1677. I am someone who describes their life as ______________________________

______________________________.

1678. I am someone who doesn't look for ______________________________

from ______________________________.

1679. I am someone who thinks miracles are ______________________________

______________________________.

1680. I am someone who gets along with ______________________________

______________________________.

1681. I am someone who doesn't like working on ______________________________

______________________________.

1682. I am someone who had their most embarrassing moment in life when ______________________________

______________________________.

1683. I am someone who respects ______________________________

but not ______________________________.

1684. I am someone who needs to ______________________________

______________________________ their daily routine.

1685. I am someone who ______________________________

______________________________ art.

1686. I am someone who is resourceful when ______________________________

______________________________.

1687. I am someone who has doubts about ______________________________

______________________________.

1688. I am someone who defines freedom as ______________________________

______________________________.

1689. I am someone who thinks competition is ______________________________

______________________________.

1690. I am someone who ______________________________

______________________________ what others think about me.

1691. I am someone who makes a ______________________________

______________________________ first impression.

1692. I am someone who almost gave up on ______________________________

but then ______________________________.

1693. I am someone who thinks ______________________________

______________________________ is a bad idea.

1694. I am someone who can't eat ______________________________

because of ______________________________.

1695. I am someone who is owed an apology from ______________________________

____.

1696. I am someone who couldn't ______________________________________

____ alone.

1697. I am someone who thinks wisdom is ________________________________

____.

1698. I am someone who used to dream of becoming ___________________________

____ then I grew up.

1699. I am someone who ____

____ follows the crowd.

1700. I am someone who stands out because of my ___________________________

____.

1701. I am someone who had to work hard to _______________________________

____.

1702. I am someone who ____

____ when I get good news.

1703. I am someone who had the most memorable kiss with ______________________

____.

1704. I am someone who would say ____________________________________

____ was my first crush.

1705. I am someone who had the best laugh of my life when _____________________

____.

1706. I am someone who thinks ____________________

____________________ is timeless.

1707. I am someone who loves to ____________________

____________________ when I'm inspired.

1708. I am someone who thinks pop culture is ____________________

____________________.

1709. I am someone who loves the smell of ____________________

____________________.

1710. I am someone who loves the sound of ____________________

____________________.

1711. I am someone who is most proud of ____________________

____________________.

1712. I am someone who ____________________

____________________ bucket list.

1713. I am someone who balances ____________________

by ____________________.

1714. I am someone who always looks ____________________

____________________.

1715. I am someone who thinks my best qualities are: ____________________

____________________.

1716. I am someone who gets picked on because of ____________________

____________________.

1717. I am someone who loves ______________________________

______________________________ on cold days.

1718. I am someone who loves ______________________________

______________________________ on hot days.

1719. I am someone who thinks people spend too much money on ______________

______________________________.

1720. I am someone who is ______________________________

______________________________ at saving money.

1721. I am someone who ______________________________

______________________________ thinks about entrepreneurship.

1722. I am someone who loves the color ______________________________

______________________________.

1723. I am someone who ______________________________

______________________________ to escape.

1724. I am someone who has had to endure ______________________________

______________________________.

1725. I am someone who has the mindset ______________________________

______________________________.

1726. I am someone who thinks ______________________________

______________________________ is dangerous.

1727. I am someone who thinks ______________________________

______________________________ should be earned.

1728. I am someone who needs to let go of ____

____.

1729. I am someone who admires ____

____.

1730. I am someone who thinks ____

____ is/are brave.

1731. I am someone who will never forget ____

____.

1732. I am someone who ____

____ my country.

1733. I am someone who ____

____ technology.

1734. I am someone who ____

____ shopping.

1735. I am someone who hates visiting ____

____.

1736. I am someone who loves visiting ____

____.

1737. I am someone who is ____

____ at telling jokes.

1738. I am someone who tells myself ____

____.

1739. I am someone who has ______________________________

______________________________ started a rumor.

1740. I am someone who thinks ______________________________

______________________________ is childish.

1741. I am someone who thinks revenge ______________________________

______________________________.

1742. I am someone who thinks ______________________________

______________________________ is an important charity.

1743. I am someone who is ______________________________

______________________________ at dancing.

1744. I am someone who loves to ______________________________

______________________________ in the winter.

1745. I am someone who loves to ______________________________

______________________________ in the summer.

1746. I am someone who thinks change is ______________________________

______________________________.

1747. I am someone who describes my core values as ______________________________

______________________________.

1748. I am someone who wants to plan for ______________________________

______________________________.

1749. I am someone who has many reasons to ______________________________

______________________________.

1750. I am someone who holds ______________________________

______________________________ to a high standard.

1751. I am someone who has put a lot of effort into ______________________________

______________________________.

1752. I am someone who will end a friendship if ______________________________

____

1753. I am someone who gets asked ______________________________

______________________________ all the time.

1754. I am someone who wants to join ______________________________

______________________________.

1755. I am someone who considers themselves a ______________________________

______________________________ driver.

1756. I am someone who ______________________________

______________________________ gives me anxiety.

1757. I am someone who thinks ______________________________

______________________________ is the worst feeling in the world.

1758. I am someone who ______________________________

______________________________ loan money to a friend.

1759. I am someone who ______________________________

______________________________ loan money to family.

1760. I am someone who ______________________________

______________________________ if I found a wallet/purse with money in it.

1761. I am someone who describes self-love as ______________________________

____.

1762. I am someone who expresses my love for others by ______________________

____.

1763. I am someone who finds it hard to express _____________________________

____ to others.

1764. I am someone who respects ____

and would never ____.

1765. I am someone who feels validated when _______________________________

____.

1766. I am someone who uses the medium of _________________________________

____ to express my creativity.

1767. I am someone who ____

____ when I feel lost.

1768. I am someone who belongs to generation ______________________________

____.

1769. I am someone who ____

____ when I'm mad at someone.

1770. I am someone who thinks insecurities are _____________________________

____

1771. I am someone who recognizes shortcomings as __________________________

____.

1772. I am someone who wants to make ______________________________

______________________________ proud.

1773. I am someone who would love to make history by ______________________________

______________________________.

1774. I am someone who wrestles with myself about ______________________________

______________________________.

1775. I am someone who would describe my alter ego as ______________________________

______________________________.

1776. I am someone who gets bursts of energy from ______________________________

______________________________.

1777. I am someone who is very enthusiastic about ______________________________

______________________________.

1778. I am someone who loves playing ______________________________

______________________________ at parties or gatherings.

1779. I am someone who ______________________________

______________________________ swimmer.

1780. I am someone who ______________________________

______________________________ running.

1781. I am someone who caused a scene once when ______________________________

______________________________.

1782. I am someone who loves the artist ______________________________

______________________________.

1783. I am someone who loves the author ______________________________

______________________________.

1784. I am someone who would love to eat food prepared by chef ______________________________

______________________________.

1785. I am someone who eats ______________________________

______________________________ when I want a late-night snack.

1786. I am someone who loves the actor ______________________________

______________________________.

1787. I am someone who loves the movie ______________________________

______________________________.

1788. I am someone who likes ______________________________

______________________________ on my pizza.

1789. I am someone who when I am wrong I will ______________________________

______________________________.

1790. I am someone who is ______________________________

______________________________ underestimated.

1791. I am someone who ______________________________

______________________________ recycles.

1792. I am someone who ______________________________

______________________________ dance/ed in the rain.

1793. I am someone who ______________________________

______________________________ climb a mountain.

1794. I am someone who ______________________________

______________________________ public speaking.

1795. I am someone who is still undecided about ______________________________

______________________________.

1796. I am someone who ______________________________

______________________________ when I want to be alone.

1797. I am someone who gets easily distracted when ______________________________

______________________________.

1798. I am someone who is a fanatic about ______________________________

______________________________.

1799. I am someone who if I wrote a piece of fan fiction it would be on ______________________________

______________________________.

1800. I am someone who ______________________________

______________________________ would make my tomorrow better.

1801. I am someone who ______________________________

______________________________ and is not a fact I share about myself.

1802. I am someone who ______________________________

______________________________ always makes me LOL.

1803. I am someone who ______________________________

when I experienced the loss of ______________________________.

1804. I am someone who doesn't think ______________________________

______________________________ is ethical.

1805. I am someone who finds ______
useful when I'm ______.

1806. I am someone who has a hard time believing in ______
______.

1807. I am someone who does ______
______ when I want to get my point across.

1808. I am someone who ______
______ follows the rules.

1809. I am someone who has always been cautious of ______
______.

1810. I am someone who ______
______ hits the snooze button.

1811. I am someone who motivates myself by ______
______.

1812. I am someone who is a ______
______ listener.

1813. I am someone who might have a chip on my shoulder about ______
______.

1814. I am someone who spends most of my time ______
______.

1815. I am someone who dreads having to ______
______.

1816. I am someone who needs a daily reminder to ______________________________

____.

1817. I am someone who occasionally suffers from ______________________________

____.

1818. I am someone who looks back on ______________________________________

____ and can laugh now.

1819. I am someone who ____

____ problem solver.

1820. I am someone who ____

____ thinks outside the box.

1821. I am someone who ____

____ is my home away from home.

1822. I am someone who regrets not dedicating enough time to ___________________

____.

1823. I am someone who wants to tell future me ____________________________

____.

1824. I am someone who sometimes fakes ______________________________________

____.

1825. I am someone who connects with people who are ________________________

____.

1826. I am someone who permits themselves to ______________________________

____.

1827. I am someone who ______________________________

______________________________ goes a long way in my book.

1828. I am someone who thinks people should ______________________________

more and ______________________________ less.

1829. I am someone who admires ______________________________

______________________________ work.

1830. I am someone who usually thinks about ______________________________

______________________________ when I first wake up.

1831. I am someone who would describe my ideal day as ______________________________

______________________________.

1832. I am someone who would describe my ideal significant other as ______________________________

______________________________.

1833. I am someone who ______________________________

______________________________ came back to bite me in the butt.

1834. I am someone who fears one day ______________________________

______________________________ will catch up to me.

1835. I am someone who feels like they are hiding from ______________________________

______________________________.

1836. I am someone who feels like ______________________________

______________________________ is an undervalued part of society.

1837. I am someone who is unlikely ______________________________

______________________________.

1838. I am someone who doesn't know me are shocked when I tell them ______

______.

1839. I am someone who hates having to explain ______

______ about myself.

1840. I am someone who is still learning to accept ______

______ is not my fault.

1841. I am someone who is slowly getting used to ______

______.

1842. I am someone who finds ______

______ daunting.

1843. I am someone who can get intimidated by ______

______.

1844. I am someone who works through my anxiety by ______

______.

1845. I am someone who thinks ______

______ is outdated.

1846. I am someone who appreciates my family's tradition of ______

______.

1847. I am someone who will pass down ______

______ to my family as it was passed down to me.

1848. I am someone who ______

fascinates me because ______.

1849. I am someone who thinks social media has a negative effect on me because ______

______.

1850. I am someone who thinks social media can have a positive effect on me if ______

______.

1851. I am someone who would describe my dream birthday party as ______

______.

1852. I am someone who thinks celebrities are ______

______ in our society.

1853. I am someone who would like to learn ______

______ from another culture.

1854. I am someone who appreciates the ______

______ of art.

1855. I am someone who appreciates the ______

______ of nature.

1856. I am someone who appreciates the ______

______ of the ocean.

1857. I am someone who is transparent about ______

______.

1858. I am someone who ______

______ practice mindfulness.

1859. I am someone who ______

______ individual differences.

1860. I am someone who if I had a theme song, it would be ______________________________

____.

1861. I am someone who holds on too tightly to ______________________________

____.

1862. I am someone who gets an adrenaline rush when ______________________________

____.

1863. I am someone who is still learning how to ______________________________

____ for myself.

1864. I am someone who doesn't want to keep looking in the rearview mirror and seeing

____.

1865. I am someone who wants to be free from ______________________________

____.

1866. I am someone who takes pride in my ______________________________

____.

1867. I am someone who classifies myself as ______________________________

____.

1868. I am someone who interprets ______________________________

____ differently than most people.

1869. I am someone who can be dramatic about ______________________________

____.

1870. I am someone who wished I had studied ______________________________

____.

1871. I am someone who keeps my distance from ______________________________
______________________________.

1872. I am someone who would never dabble in ______________________________
for fear of ______________________________.

1873. I am someone who thinks the best gifts are ones ______________________________
______________________________.

1874. I am someone who is grappling coming to terms with ______________________________
______________________________.

1875. I am someone who gave up on ______________________________
______________________________ and still regret it.

1876. I am someone who just finished reading ______________________________
______________________________.

1877. I am someone who just finished binging on ______________________________
______________________________.

1878. I am someone who had to step away from ______________________________
so I could ______________________________.

1879. I am someone who wants to rekindle ______________________________
______________________________.

1880. I am someone who wished they were not ______________________________
______________________________.

1881. I am someone who usually goes to sleep feeling ______________________________
______________________________.

1882. I am someone who has had a recent high that ______________________________

______________________________.

1883. I am someone who has had a recent low that ______________________________

______________________________.

1884. I am someone who ______________________________

______________________________ excites me about the future.

1885. I am someone who ______________________________

______________________________ terrifies me about the future.

1886. I am someone who learned ______________________________

______________________________ from successes I've had in my life.

1887. I am someone who ______________________________

______________________________ greatly impacts my mood.

1888. I am someone who needs to reframe my image of ______________________________

______________________________.

1889. I am someone who needs to show more compassion to ______________________________

______________________________.

1890. I am someone who feels most in tune with myself when ______________________________

______________________________.

1891. I am someone who has been a victim of ______________________________

______________________________.

1892. I am someone who has high standards when it comes to ______________________________

______________________________.

1893. I am someone who ______________________________

______________________________ have an affair with a married person.

1894. I am someone who has restrictions for ______________________________

that are necessary because of ______________________________.

1895. I am someone who is drawn to ______________________________

______________________________ in other people.

1896. I am someone who ______________________________

______________________________ causes me to act out sometimes.

1897. I am someone who needs to confess ______________________________

to clear the air with ______________________________.

1898. I am someone who has the song ______________________________

______________________________ always on repeat.

1899. I am someone who if I was in charge of the country where I live would ______________

______________________________.

1900. I am someone who ______________________________

______________________________ more than I get back from others.

1901. I am someone who despite everything that I've been through still believe ______________

______________________________.

1902. I am someone who wants ______________________________

to take accountability for ______________________________.

1903. I am someone who thought my life felt like a soap opera when ______________

______________________________.

1904. I am someone who ______________________________

is my favorite social media app because ______________________________.

1905. I am someone who loves when people tell me ______________________________

______________________________.

1906. I am someone who ______________________________

______________________________ is the most beautiful thing in my life right now.

1907. I am someone who is evolving as a person by ______________________________

______________________________.

1908. I am someone who stays grounded by ______________________________

______________________________.

1909. I am someone who ______________________________

______________________________ still friends with my childhood friends.

1910. I am someone who likes to keep ______________________________

______________________________ for keepsakes and memorabilia.

1911. I am someone who is still trying to repair my relationship with ______________________________

from ______________________________.

1912. I am someone who is thinking about rekindling ______________________________

______________________________.

1913. I am someone who the quickest way to irritate is ______________________________

______________________________.

1914. I am someone who wishes people could understand ______________________________

______________________________ about me.

1915. I am someone who wishes people knew ______________________________

______________________________ about me.

1916. I am someone who is living life on my own terms by ______________________________

______________________________.

1917. I am someone who if my life was a movie the genre it would be is ______________________________

______________________________.

1918. I am someone who if my life was a movie I would want the actor ______________________________

______________________________ to play me.

1919. I am someone who if my life was a movie the title would be ______________________________

______________________________.

1920. I am someone who has to make hard choices with my most recent hardest choice

being ______________________________.

1921. I am someone who the hardest change for me to make was ______________________________

______________________________.

1922. I am someone who the hardest bad habit to break was ______________________________

______________________________.

1923. I am someone who pop culture has influenced my personality by ______________________________

______________________________.

1924. I am someone who the media has influenced my outlook by ______________________________

______________________________.

1925. I am someone who my current environment has shaped me by ______________________________

______________________________.

1926. I am someone who wants to improve dialogue with ____________________

____.

1927. I am someone who wants to train for ____________________

____.

1928. I am someone who appreciates ____________________

____________________________________ about myself.

1929. I am someone who ____________________

____________________________________ marry a friend's ex.

1910. I am someone who ____________________

____________________________________ marry a former enemy.

1931. I am someone who ____________________

____________________________ marry a person 10 years older than me.

1932. I am someone who ____________________

____________________________ turned out to be a blessing in disguise.

1933. I am someone who experimented with ____________________

and quickly learned ____________________________.

1934. I am someone who was on cloud 9 when ____________________

____.

1935. I am someone who decided to bury the hatchet with ____________________

to benefit ____________________________________.

1936. I am someone who likes to blow off steam by ____________________

____.

1937. I am someone who went through a dark period in my life but then ______________________

______________________ was the light at the end of the tunnel I needed.

1938. I am someone who is trying to enjoy the best of both worlds and have ______________________

______________________ simultaneously.

1939. I am someone who learned a lesson that the "grass is not always greener" when I

______________________.

1940. I am someone who jumped on the bandwagon of ______________________

and it made me ______________________.

1941. I am someone who puts their heart and soul into ______________________

______________________.

1942. I am someone who sometimes feels like I need to be rescued from ______________________

______________________.

1943. I am someone who always has a good time when I ______________________

______________________.

1944. I am someone who would rate my physical fitness as ______________________

______________________.

1945. I am someone who wants to be liberated from ______________________

______________________.

1946. I am someone who ______________________

______________________ is like chicken soup for my soul.

1947. I am someone who ______________________

a muse for ______________________.

1948. I am someone who has been ostracized before for ______________________________

____.

1949. I am someone who thinks the most important disease that needs to have a cure is ____

____.

1950. I am someone who ____

____ scars.

1951. I am someone who considered these potential baby names for my children __________

____.

1952. I am someone who can be stubborn about __________________________________

____.

1953. I am someone who ____

____ danced in the rain.

1954. I am someone who____

____ took a leap of faith.

1955. I am someone who never stops trying to __________________________________

____.

1956. I am someone who refuses to allow ____________________________________

____ to steal my joy.

1957. I am someone who refuses to allow ____________________________________

____ to affect my mood.

1958. I am someone who sometimes allows ___________________________________

____ to live rent free inside my head.

1959. I am someone who hopes my children do not inherit my ______________________

____.

1960. I am someone who sometimes has to convince myself that I deserve ____________

____.

1961. I am someone who ______________________________

______________________________________ common sense.

1962. I am someone who isn't afraid to stand up to ______________________

____.

1963. I am someone who hides away from the world when ____________________

____.

1964. I am someone who thinks your past ______________________________

____.

1965. I am someone who keeps my mind sharp by ________________________

____.

1966. I am someone who would describe my decorating style as ______________

____.

1967. I am someone who thinks ______________________________

______________________ is the most important writer of this century.

1968. I am someone who has used the excuse ______________________

______________________________ to get out of work or school.

1969. I am someone who ______________________________

______________________________________ on time.

1970. I am someone who thinks the sexiest people are those who ____________________

____.

1971. I am someone who is trying to live consciously by ____________________

____.

1972. I am someone who ____

______________________________ brings out the best in me.

1973. I am someone who ____

____________________________________ piercings.

1974. I am someone who had to learn the hard way about ____________________

____.

1975. I am someone who ____

paper books and ______________________________ electronic books.

1976. I am someone who thinks libraries are ______________________________

____.

1977. I am someone who gained a lot of insight to ______________________________

through ____.

1978. I am someone who has childlike excitement when ____________________

____.

1979. I am someone who ____

______________________________ is a way to lose my trust.

1980. I am someone who had to choose between ______________________________

and that decision left me ____.

1981. I am someone who is not picky about ______________________________

______________________________.

1982. I am someone who ______________________________

spirit and a ______________________________ soul.

1983. I am someone who has an inner voice that is always telling me ______________________________

______________________________.

1984. I am someone who has annoying reoccurring thoughts about ______________________________

______________________________.

1985. I am someone who ______________________________

______________________________ an organ donor.

1986. I am someone who would rate my dancing skills as ______________________________

______________________________.

1987. I am someone who has always wanted to be included in ______________________________

______________________________.

1988. I am someone who joined ______________________________

______________________________ when I was a kid.

1989. I am someone who thinks ______________________________

______________________________ are the most terrifying insects on the planet.

1990. I am someone who would love to have a ______________________________

______________________________ accent.

1991. I am someone who thinks thinks hunting is ______________________________

______________________________.

1992. I am someone who thinks fishing is ______________________________

______________________________.

1993. I am someone who thinks bars are ______________________________

______________________________.

1994. I am someone who ______________________________

______________________________ a dating app.

1995. I am someone who ______________________________

______________________________ crash/crashed a wedding.

1996. I am someone who ______________________________

______________________________ crash/crashed a party.

1997. I am someone who thinks you can learn a lot from ______________________________

______________________________ just by paying attention.

1998. I am someone who thinks karaoke is ______________________________

______________________________.

1999. I am someone who wants to be remembered as ______________________________

______________________________.

2000. I am someone who when I get to the end of my life want to look back and know ______

______________________________.

2001. I am someone who gained so much insight from ______________________________

______________________________.

2002. I am someone who refuses to accept ______________________________

______________________________ in any relationship.

2003. I am someone who ______________________________

______________________________ stops to smell the roses.

2004. I am someone who would describe my current look as ______________________________

______________________________.

2005. I am someone who always tries to emulate ______________________________

______________________________.

2006. I am someone who would ______________________________

______________________________ if I found a lost kitten/puppy.

2007. I am someone who never likes to ______________________________

before bedtime because ______________________________.

2008. I am someone who would describe my inner circle as ______________________________

______________________________.

2009. I am someone who thinks ______________________________

______________________________ was one big hoax.

2010. I am someone who tries too hard to ______________________________

only to be left feeling ______________________________.

2011. I am someone who would have love to be born in ______________________________

time period because ______________________________.

2012. I am someone who feels gaslit when ______________________________

______________________________.

2013. I am someone who is still dealing with backlash from ______________________________

______________________________.

2014. I am someone who isn't afraid to ______________________________

even if it means ______________________________.

2015. I am someone who never wants to make an uninformed decision when it comes to

______________________________.

2016. I am someone who building the courage to ______________________________

______________________________.

2017. I am someone who treasures ______________________________

______________________________ even if others can't see the value.

2018. I am someone who always tries to repurpose ______________________________

______________________________.

2019. I am someone who worries AI will ______________________________

______________________________.

2020. I am someone who thinks ______________________________

______________________________ will happen in 100 years.

2021. I am someone who is always changing my mind about ______________________________

______________________________.

2022. I am someone who has ______________________________

______________________________ in common with a celebrity.

2023. I am someone who would love to be a fly on the wall in ______________________________

______________________________ house.

2024. I am someone who embraces the power of ______________________________

______________________________.

2025. I am someone who learned more from ______________________________

______________________________ than I ever learned in school.

2026. I am someone who is always the ______________________________

______________________________ at parties.

2027. I am someone who can never shut up about ______________________________

______________________________.

2028. I am someone who would never want to be challenged to a ______________________________

______________________________.

2029. I am someone who welcomes the challenge of ______________________________

______________________________.

2030. I am someone who connects on a deeper level to ______________________________

______________________________.

2031. I am someone who would ______________________________

______________________________ if I wanted to cause a scene.

2032. I am someone who respects the process of ______________________________

______________________________.

2033. I am someone who makes a wish when ______________________________

______________________________.

2034. I am someone who holds themselves accountable for ______________________________

______________________________ daily.

2035. I am someone who sees themselves in ______________________________

______________________________.

2036. I am someone who feels ____________________

____________________ when I dwell on the past.

2037. I am someone who feels ____________________

____________________ when I think too much about the future.

2038. I am someone who never slows down when ____________________

____________________.

2039. I am someone who was haunted by the urban legend (scary story) of ____________________

____________________ when I was younger.

2040. I am someone who wanted to ____________________

____________________ in school but never got the chance.

2041. I am someone who love to be serenaded by ____________________

____________________.

2042. I am someone who describes their current era (season of life) as ____________________

____________________.

2043. I am someone who would freak out if I found ____________________

____________________ hiding under my bed.

2044. I am someone who realizes as I get older I need more ____________________

____________________ in my life.

2045. I am someone who used to never appreciate ____________________

____________________ but as I grow wiser I realize the value.

2046. I am someone who will never deny ____________________

____________________ to someone who asks me.

2047. I am someone who feels awkward when I wear ______________________________

____.

2048. I am some one who feels overpowered by ______________________________

when ____.

2049. I am someone my family would say is most likely to ______________________________

____ at a family reunion.

2050. I am someone who is deeply impacted by ______________________________

____ each time I think about it.

2051. I am someone who was heavily influenced by ______________________________

and it helped shape my ____.

2052. I am someone who would never ______________________________

____ on a vacation.

2053. I am someone who wants to leave a mark on this world by ______________________________

____.

2054. I am someone who tries to salvage ______________________________

____ if I can.

2055. I am someone who would probably do ______________________________

____ at my next class reunion.

2056. I am someone who ______________________________

____ detention in school.

2057. I am someone who thinks the worst punishment my parents ever gave me was ______________________________

____.

2058. I am someone who thinks the best reward my parents ever gave me was ____.

2059. I am someone who feels like I lose a piece of myself when ____.

2060. I am someone who ______________________________________ makes me feel powerful and gives me a take charge mentality.

2061. I am someone who thinks you can learn a lot from ____ just by paying attention.

2062. I am someone who thinks karaoke is ____.

2063. I am someone who thinks true crime documentaries and podcasts ____.

2064. I am someone who ____ remakes of classic movies.

2065. I am someone who ____ nature documentaries.

2066. I am someone who thinks ____ is the best voiceover actor.

2067. I am someone who thinks privacy in today's world is ____.

2068. I am someone who feels like crap when ____.

2069. I am someone who would call myself ______________________________

______________________________ if I ever became a rapper.

2070. I am someone who thinks you should ______________________________

______________________________ earlier in life.

2071. I am someone who wasted too much time on ______________________________

and it cost me ______________________________.

2072. I am someone who subscribes to the philosophy of ______________________________

______________________________.

2073. I am someone who never wants to measure the fullness of life by ______________________________

______________________________.

2074. I am someone who can't imagine a world without ______________________________

______________________________.

2075. I am someone who tries to lead by example when it comes to ______________________________

______________________________.

2076. I am someone who is always reevaluating ______________________________

______________________________ on a day-to-day basis.

2077. I am someone who is prone to ______________________________

when ______________________________.

2078. I am someone who has always believed one day I would ______________________________

______________________________.

2079. I am someone who ______________________________ to follow

______________________________ footsteps.

2080. I am someone who has to remind myself constantly that ______________________

____.

2081. I am someone who felt a strong calling on my life to ______________________

____.

2082. I am someone who made a promise to ______________________

that I would ____.

2083. I am someone who tries to warn others about ______________________

____.

2084. I am someone who tries to warn others about ______________________

____.

2085. I am someone who can easily detect when someone ______________________

____.

2086. I am someone who often exaggerates ______________________

so I can ____.

2087. I am someone who has trouble surrendering control of ______________________

when ____.

2088. I am someone who once told a lie so big it ______________________

____.

2089. I am someone who lied about ______________________

so I could ____.

2090. I am someone who learned the value of ______________________

when ____.

2091. I am someone who has a bad habit of ______________________________ to other people.

2092. I am someone who measures ______________________________ by ______________________________.

2093. I am someone who hates when people accuse me of ______________________________.

2094. I am someone who sometimes overshares when it comes to ______________________________.

2095. I am someone who tries to make memories by ______________________________.

2096. I am someone who there's a thin line between ______________________________.

2097. I am someone who is not confident about ______________________________ when it comes to the future.

2098. I am someone who would probably ______________________________ if I was ever abducted by aliens.

2099. I am someone who thinks dating apps are ______________________________.

2100. I am someone who considers "me time" to be filled with ______________________________.

2101. I am someone who never underestimates the power of ______________________________.

2102. I am someone who wishes someone will revolutionize ______________________

____.

2103. I am someone who keeps ______________________________

______________________________ closely guarded.

2104. I am someone who tries to justify ______________________________

____.

2105. I am someone who knew from an early age that I ______________________

____.

2106. I am someone who finds it impossible to have fun if ______________________

____.

2107. I am someone who describes their artistic style and creativity as ______________

____.

2108. I am someone who gets carried away with ______________________________

______________________________ if I am not careful.

2109. I am someone who would ______________________________

______________________ if I feel like someone is following me.

2110. I am someone who can't let go of the idea one day ______________________

____.

2111. I am someone who was on the receiving end of karma when ______________

____.

2112. I am someone who use to dabble in ______________________________

but now I dabble in ______________________________.

2113. I am someone who loves to make other people ______________________________

______________________________.

2114. I am someone who keeps things interesting by always ______________________________

______________________________.

2115. I am someone who loves revisiting the memory of ______________________________

______________________________.

2116. I am someone who never thought I would get caught up in ______________________________

______________________________.

2117. I am someone who can't imagine a world where ______________________________

______________________________ doesn't exist.

2118. I am someone who used to carry the shame of ______________________________

______________________________.

2119. I am someone who would describe their RBF as ______________________________

______________________________.

2120. I am someone who gives off main character energy by ______________________________

______________________________.

2121. I am someone who would allow ______________________________

______________________________ to write one chapter of my story.

2122. I am someone who regrets hesitating when ______________________________

______________________________.

2123. I am someone who thinks about ______________________________

______________________________ when I look at the stars in the sky.

2124. I am someone who loves getting my hands dirty by ______________________________

____.

2125. I am someone who wouldn't change a thing about ______________________________

____.

2126. I am someone who knows I am capable of ______________________________

____.

2127. I am someone who always makes a wish when I ______________________________

____.

2128. I am someone who worry about ______________________________

______________________________ if I had to make a speech in front of a large crowd.

2129. I am someone who would make a good contestant/competitor on ______________

____.

2130. I am someone who resonates with ______________________________

____ on a deeper level.

2131. I am someone who feels out of touch with ______________________________

____.

2132. I am someone who loves to revisit ______________________________

____ from my childhood.

2133. I am someone who tries to hide my emotions by ______________________________

____.

2134. I am someone who my friends expect to ______________________________

____.

Piccadilly®